The Approaching Country

An Expedition to Messiah's Coming Homeland

Clifford A. Jennings

CubitHound Publishing
Highland, Maryland 20777

Verses marked NASB are taken from the New American Standard Bible®. ©1960, 1962, 1963, 1968, 1971, 1973, 1975, 1977, 1995 by the Lockman Foundation.

Verses marked NIV are taken from The Holy Bible, New International Version®. ©1973, 1978, 1984, 2011 by the International Bible Society. Quotes here are taken from the 1984 version.

Verses marked NJPS are taken from The Jewish Bible, Tanakh, The Holy Scriptures, The New JPS Translation According to the Traditional Hebrew Text. ©1985 by the Jewish Publication Society.

Verses marked KJV are taken from the King James Version of the Bible, while those marked ASV are from the Authorized Standard Version of the Bible.

Citations marked ISBE are taken from the International Standard Bible Encyclopedia. James Orr, editor, Grand Rapids, MI: Eerdmans Publishing Company, 1939. Citations marked "Strong's" are taken from The New Strong's Exhaustive Concordance of the Bible, James Strong, editor, Nashville, TN: Thomas Nelson Publishers, 1990; first published 1890.

Cover art by Leah Rose Jennings.

All illustrations (with the exception of certain backgrounds or other elements as explained in footnotes) are by the author. Color & higher-resolution versions of all figures are available for download on www.EarthAwaits.com.

The Approaching Country
An Expedition to Messiah's Coming Homeland

Published by CubitHound Publishing, Highland, MD 20777
www.EarthAwaits.com

ISBN-10 0990389405
ISBN-13 978-0-9903894-0-8
Library of Congress Control Number: 2014908562

To my wife, Linda.

Your loving encouragement, over all these years, has enabled this effort; and I truly thank you from the bottom of my heart.

Acknowledgments

My sincere gratitude goes to Linda Jennings, Ben and Mary Jean Jennings, and Kathy Himebaugh, for their encouragement and editing assistance in this work.

Contents

List of Figures

Preface

If we have a sincere faith based on what God has spoken in the Bible, we share a hope for a life beyond this one in a realm created by the Lord that far transcends the world we know. With the Scriptures as our basis, we understand that we'll all die at some point, and go to one of two places; and no one wants to go to the darker destination. So, whether Jew or Christian, of whatever genre, I think it's safe to say that we hold this overarching goal in common: *Heaven.*

There is, however, another coming "other-world" taught in the Bible, a positive and truly wonderful one; and it is not Heaven. Rather, it is the prophesied era of *our current Earth* wherein God's Anointed[1] will come to reign as literal King of kings in *this* world, bringing healing and harmony throughout.

We do not emphasize this time and place nearly as much as we do Heaven. Perhaps this is because Heaven is the aspiration for all who believe in the Lord Adonai, throughout all history; whereas participation in Messiah's coming realm seems a matter of being in the right place (spiritually and physically) at the right time. We who believe in God's Word look to an eternal home with Him in Heaven, and always have. By comparison, an interest in His future dominion *here* may seem to be in the academic arena of Biblical prophecy and eschatology[2], and therefore optional, esoteric, and even perhaps uncomfortable.

Even so, I would like to point out why, in addition to keeping our hope in Heaven vibrant, it is also a very good thing to understand this Kingdom coming to earth, and keep an eye on what God is doing around the corner in world events ahead. For example, these subjects of Heaven and Messiah's approaching dominion are in fact very much intertwined. Both comprise domains under direct rule of the Lord Almighty, reflecting His holiness, order, vitality, love, and prosperity. If one can observe and learn something from one of those jurisdictions, one is to some degree informed of the other. Indeed, not much is said in the Bible about Heaven; but a *lot* is said about the next earthly age to come. If we can grasp some of the factuality and tangibility of the latter, we can absorb some of the same for the former.

It is also good to remind ourselves that God's intent is to bring His Anointed King, His Son in fact, to defeat the Enemy and reign victoriously over not only the Holy Land, but His entire creation. By examining foreseen details of

[1] Hebrew: *mashiach*; Greek: *christos*; English versions of the two words: *messiah* and *christ*, respectively. In this work, the terms *Anointed [One]*, *Christ*, *Messiah* and *Mashiach* will be used interchangeably.

[2] The study of things to come, especially in regards to Biblical prophecies of consummating events.

that reign, even small aspects of it, we are reminding ourselves of that future victory, and – in a real sense – celebrating it in advance, to God's glory.

Another reason for this investigation is that if we *do* in fact find ourselves at the right place – or rather, time – in the chronology of God's program through history, our next stop may *not* be Heaven, but instead the coming King's administration over a creation healed and rejuvenated. Christians throughout the world often pray, "*Thy kingdom come… on Earth, as it is in Heaven.*"[3] Similarly, I expect that many Jews long for and pray for the day when their people are at last "*the head and not the tail.*"[4]At some point, such believers will get what they've been praying for. So an additional reason for taking on this journey is simply to have a better idea of what to expect. Not a perfect idea by any means; just a better one.

True, most folks who have ever lived will not directly experience the coming day of Messiah-Christ. Yet many people will. Some sense that the time is drawing near; and some are apprehensive of transitional events prophesied to occur just prior. This is not a book about the "end times," the "Antichrist, "or "Armageddon." It is, however, a study of circumstances that are certainly "post-apocalyptic": for they transpire after the "revealing" of the King, in the context of His wise and powerful reign. So while we are not going into details of transitional events before then, we will gain knowledge of the Kingdom on the other side. That understanding may well serve as a needed encouragement in days ahead.

Whether Messiah's coming is distant, soon, or *very* soon, only He knows for sure. But we can appreciate that he, like His earthly ancestor David, will establish a mighty and wonderful Kingdom beyond our imagination, and to the benefit of all humankind. Based on clues granted us in Scripture though, try to imagine we shall. The expedition ahead is to a land that *will* literally exist on this Earth, to a geographic region that people like you and I will experience with all their senses. In a sense, we are embarking on a treasure hunt for hard information about that territory on the horizon, seeking after riches in understanding of the marvels our Lord will accomplish in this creation, in days ahead.

Beyond this present expedition, further ones are invited by the Scriptures, with just as much prophetic clues and encouragement. These topics include the coming Mountain of the Lord; the great City of Messiah's government; the glorious Temple; and the rejuvenated world at that time. We will limit this exploration though to the native country of Messiah, Israel, as God's Word describes it to be in days ahead. Some parts might seem detailed, to the degree that you feel inclined to just scan it for now. That's fine. You may want to use the footnotes for further study, or skip them. Feel free to do either, and take this

[3] Matthew 6:10.

[4] Deuteronomy 28:13.

tour at your own pace and in your own way. The main thing is that we come away from this journey with a basic understanding of the Holy Land on the horizon, and – especially – the focal "dedicated district" at its core. And if we can better glimpse the wonder of God's Word, if we can more viscerally sense how His purposes enfold us, if we are strengthened in our faith along the way, so much the better!

It is my hope that our little reconnaissance will be as intriguing for you as it has been to me. If the things we learn here assist our belief and resolve, perhaps the shared understanding will bring us all closer together under the One God, our Creator and Master, Adonai.

Cliff Jennings
Highland, Maryland
May 2014

Chapter 1: Initial Preparations

"I make known the end from the beginning, from ancient times, what is still to come. I say: My purpose will stand, and I will do all that I please."

Isaiah 46:10, NIV

... the prophets have inquired and searched diligently... what manner of time... the glory that should follow.

1 Peter 1:10- 11, KJV, excerpts

"... I am watching to see that my word is fulfilled."

Jeremiah 1:12b, NIV

A Hidden Land on the Horizon

We've seen, read and heard many of them: stories about a secret land that no-one knows about except a few characters – some of them good guys, some of them not so good. Motivating everyone in the plot is not just the fact of that land, but what it contains: a true treasure, worth any amount of effort to discover and obtain.

These stories are plentiful because something about them speaks to us. Wouldn't it be awesome to go on such a journey? Of course! We all want to discover something big, to understand something secret. And we're all wired, to one degree or another, for some quest that breaks us out of the usual patterns of our life. So we enjoy our adventure movies and books, whatever their genre or setting. At the same time, we know it's all safe. We can read a chapter and put the book down. We can watch the show and go to bed.

There is, however, a story in the Bible that's just as compelling as our adventure tales. It is a story about things that will happen here on this earth, perhaps in our lifetime. It is a story about places and events just as real and factual as anything we experience, but told in advance. Spicing things up, to put it mildly, are the dangers involved: for sometimes information and motivation are dangerous.

But why would this story be so secret? Because, like many prophecies that still await their outworking, the Lord has chosen to distribute the information to us in various Biblical clues that, only with His help and in His timing, can be brought together into a readable image. Also, an interested mind is also required: for a secret can be kept a secret through disinterest and oversight. Since an overwhelming (yet often overlooked or dismissed) body of clues is available on the subject, we can at least pay attention. And with God's help, we will gain some insight into things that are not exactly in the arena of regular teaching.

What is this story about? Just this: the *land* of the coming *King*. It has to do with what we often call "The Holy Land," the country of Israel. But in view of what the Bible says about this region in the coming Day of Messiah's reign, we might as well be talking about – in some very important senses – a territory that does not yet exist. Yet sometime soon, it will.

Potential Dangers

As with any good adventure story, this journey has its dangers to be reckoned with. But unlike fictional tales, these risks are real, and we should be aware of them[5].

For example, whenever we take seriously what God says about His future intentions in "our" realm on Earth, we set ourselves up as targets for ridicule. It might be "safe" to believe that He led His people Israel out of Egypt in the past. It is a different matter to consider that the same God might do the same thing once more, in this same world, but on a much larger scale. But if scorn comes, we must remind ourselves that we're not making this up, nor are we hiding from the facts. The Lord does not change[6]; His Word will perform all He intends[7], yet He will take care of His people throughout[8].

Another point. Particularly in western cultures, there seems to be an eagerness to dismiss God's declarations on future events as myth. This attitude towards eschatology permeates educational institutions and the various secular media; and it increasingly involves a stance against anyone who takes the Lord at His Word. If we explore the Holy Land to come as God describes, and say anything about it, reactions will occur; and with them will be potential threats, alienation and intimidation. Yet we need to hold to what *God*, not man, says about the future, for only God is in the driver's seat of history. Our faith must be strong enough, and our skin thick enough, to withstand the doubts of those with little or no faith, and remain loving in word and deed towards them.

Here is another key issue. In any exploration of Messiah's dominion, one must resolve for one's self the special role of the nation of Israel, accepting that God's promises and declarations in the "Old" Testament are confirmed in the "New" are unbreakable[9]. Further, the New Testament cannot be severed it from its roots, in the covenant with the nation of Israel[10].

---

[5] "*...in order that Satan might not outwit us. For we are not unaware of his schemes*" (2 Corinthians 2:11, NIV).

[6] Numbers 23:19; Malachi 3:6.

[7] Isaiah 55:11.

[8] E.g., Romans 8:28.

[9] E.g., Romans 11:29.

[10] Romans 11.

Over and over, in both the First[11] Testament and New, we see that the literal nation of Israel is central to the Lord's interventions in history *and in the next era to come.* Studies such as the one before us, almost by definition, therefore invite the angst and anger of those against Israel (and her supporters). This topic of Messiah's Land, even if based on a strictly technical analysis of Biblical material, is therefore potentially inflammatory. But God invites us to see what He will perform in all this, no matter who believes or not; and we should not be frightened away from the examination.

Finally, we are, in effect, invading the Enemy's territory, by looking forward to a creation freed of his despoiling, and made to blossom under the reign of our Creator and Savior. The "serpent" will not easily give up his holdings, even at the level of intellectual understanding. It's all a threat to him. But as with all these potential threats, our defense is the Lord Himself. We can abide under the shelter of His wings; we can run to Him as our fortress; we can dwell within Him, as our Temple and City. Though the dangers and potential ambushes in this expedition are real, we can rest in knowing that our King will keep us safe, as we abide in Him.

Vital Equipment

The Mysterious Map

There are few things to pack before we move out, beginning with our map: God's holy Word. We will be using a variety of ancient Biblical texts that either directly speak about Messiah's coming country, or implicitly reflect on it.

Biblical prophecies related to pending events can, however, be downright mysterious. Sometimes they have been shrouded with interpretations based more on tradition and politics than on the internal evidence of the Word. Sometimes there is a perception of myth, due often to the work of "false prophets" over the centuries crying "the end is near," when it really wasn't. All this adds to the confusion.

---

[11] In this study, the term "First Testament" will generally replace that of "Old Testament." Though the covenant inaugurated under Moses is called "old" (e.g., 2 Corinthians 3:14) because it gave way to its fulfilling referent in Messiah's sacrifice, the Scriptures involved are in no way "old" or defunct. Indeed, Jesus Himself said that not one least stroke of the pen in those writings would fail to be fulfilled (Matthew 5:18).

Then, there is ambiguity due to division amongst believers, with some prophecies speaking to the "end times"[12] having become quite controversial, with camps of interpretation and hard lines drawn between them. For example, one group might believe that the faithful will be "raptured" to Heaven a few years before Messiah's coming, while another group believes the "tribulation" to be unavoidable for all the faithful[13]. Such division adds to the obscurity of the topic.

But with manmade occlusions such as these, is God's Word at fault? Absolutely not. For the very One who gave us the Ten Commandments is He that gave mankind the prophetic passages as well, to be understood for *His* purposes, and in *His* timing. Where we tend to get into trouble is when we substitute *our* purposes and *our* timing for "His." But no prophetic misinterpretation, whether major or minor, historical or current or future, can prevent or alter what the Lord has declared He will accomplish.

> *I make known the end from the beginning, from ancient times, what is still to come. I say: My purpose will stand, and I will do all that I please.*
> *Isaiah 46:10, NIV*

> *As the rain and the snow come down from heaven, and do not return to it without watering the earth and making it bud and flourish, so that it yields seed for the sower and bread for the eater, 11 so is* ***my word*** *that goes out from my mouth:* ***It will not return to me empty, but will accomplish what I desire and achieve the purpose for which I sent it.***
> *Isaiah 55:10-11, NIV*

> *"...* ***I am watching to see that my word is fulfilled."***
> *Jeremiah 1:12b, NIV*

> *"Is not my word like fire," declares the LORD, "and* ***like a hammer that breaks a rock in pieces?"***
> *Jeremiah 23:29, NIV*

> *Heaven and earth will pass away, but* ***my words will never pass away.***
> *Matthew 24:35, NIV*

---

[12] That is, the prophesied transition period from this age to that of Messiah's reign.

[13] Fortunately, this investigation doesn't require a settling of the "tribulation" question. Instead, we will push chronologically beyond that very brief period, looking toward the *purpose* of that transitional time: the glorious kingdom of Messiah brought to this planet, in fulfillment of God's many promises.

As in ancient times, so it is today, and will be tomorrow: not everyone gives regard to the Lord's Word[14], or the necessity for it to accomplish what it was released to perform. But neither disregard nor misunderstanding can hold back its outworking.

In the mean time, it behooves us to humbly trust our Lord and rely upon the veracity of His Word. True, God does not guarantee comprehension of all the quite real mysteries that His Word contains, for many passages have been deliberately "sealed up" by Him, their understanding awaiting His appointed time[15]. Yet even in regard to the enigmatic passages, special blessings await those that honestly seek out His intentions therein[16].

So we must hold fast to this ultimate treasure map, the mighty Word of God, for it remains the only sure means by which to decipher anything about the future. Yes, its pending prophecies are mysterious; and yes, often misunderstood or dismissed, in part or in whole. But respect it we must, study it we must, if we are to make any headway in the challenge before us here. God's Word, His map for us all, is therefore the first thing we "pack" for our expedition.

Body Armor

Every treasure hunt worth pursuing is bound to attract competition and conflict. There is ever the enemy intent on stealing the riches while harming those acting with the higher motives. In this story, the Enemy wishes not only to steal glory for himself away from Messiah, but make sure *we* do not discover the facts about His glorious realm to come. The last thing Satan wants to hear is people discussing proofs of his downfall.

Since we are now expecting some of this spiritual conflict along the way, we need to arm ourselves with certain defensive and protective gear. Here is what the Apostle Paul taught:

> *Finally, my brethren, be strong in the Lord, and in the power of his might. 11* ***Put on the whole armour of God****, that ye may be able to stand against the wiles of the devil. 12 For we wrestle not against flesh and blood, but against principalities, against powers, against the rulers of the darkness of this world, against spiritual wickedness in high places.*

---

[14] E.g., 2 Peter 3:4 ("Where is this 'coming' he promised? Ever since our fathers died, everything goes on as it has since the beginning of creation" - NIV); see also Ezekiel 12:22-23.

[15] See Daniel 8:26 & 9:24, and Revelation 10:4, vs. Revelation 22:10.

[16] E.g., Isaiah 66:2; Revelation 1:3, 22:7.

> *13 Wherefore take unto you* **the whole armour of God**, *that ye may be able to withstand in the evil day, and having done all, to stand. 14 Stand therefore, having your* **loins girt about with truth**, *and having on the* **breastplate of righteousness**; *15 And your* **feet shod with the preparation of the gospel of peace**; *16 Above all, taking the* **shield of faith**, *wherewith ye shall be able to quench all the fiery darts of the wicked.*
> *Ephesians 6:10-16, KJV*

Though the application of these verses will have to be left up to you, it is clear that these elements of armor are all the more important as we move into realms of our Lord's coming victory. For this story is a twofold threat to the Enemy: as geographic proof of his failure in conquering Israel, and as a symbolic proof of his utterly doomed fight against God's Anointed. Whether appreciated as actual or symbolic though, these are territories that the Enemy will not give up easily.

Our Primary Weapon

Paul's teaching goes on (in verse 17) to mention one weapon: "*the sword of the Spirit, which is the word of God.*" In our somewhat dangerous expedition, if there is a spiritual counterpart to a gun or whip worn by Indiana Jones, it is this Sword of the Lord. In addition to being our map, God's Word is also our defense when the Enemy attacks. For example, when doubt or depression is thrown at us, reciting praise-Psalms out loud is an excellent counterattack.

Another way to wield that Sword is to have certain key truths handy, to bring out and remind one's self of and throw into the Enemy's face – but with prayer[17]. Certainly there are innumerable candidate verses, and you might have some favorites. Given the nature of this journey though, I would like to suggest this list:

- What God intends He first proclaims: *Surely the Sovereign Lord does nothing without revealing his plan to his servants the prophets* (Amos 3:7, NIV).

- What God proclaims must happen: *so is my word that goes out from my mouth: It will not return to me empty, but will accomplish what I desire and achieve the purpose for which I sent it* (Isaiah 55:11, NIV).

[17] And not with pride: Jude 9.

- What God announces cannot be prevented: *I make known the end from the beginning, from ancient times, what is still to come. I say: My purpose will stand, and I will do all that I please* (Isaiah 46:10, NIV).

- What God speaks forth always has its effect: "*Is not my word like fire," declares the Lord, "and like a hammer that breaks a rock in pieces?*" (Jeremiah 23:29, NIV).

- What God foretells may be concealed for a time, and revealed only when He decides: *For you this whole vision is nothing but words sealed in a scroll. And if you give the scroll to someone who can read, and say to him, "Read this, please," he will answer, "I can't; it is sealed"* (Isaiah 29:11, NIV). "*The vision of the evenings and mornings that has been given you is true, but seal up the vision, for it concerns the distant future*" (Daniel 8:26b, NIV).

- What God declares will be understood in His timing: *But you, Daniel, close up and seal the words of the scroll until the time of the end*" (Daniel 12:4a, NIV). *Then he told me, "Do not seal up the words of the prophecy of this book, because the time is near*" (Revelation 22:10, NIV).

Though the study ahead is imperfect, though our comprehension is not faultless, God's Word is flawless and immutable. In fact, it is a living force for His purposes[18]. In the journey ahead, we will find verses such as those just cited to be helpful elements of our primary weapon, the Sword of the Spirit.

A Key Measuring Device

The next thing to pack is a quite literal item – that is, if you had one handy, as people did in the past, and will in the future. It is a tool, a measuring device. Ezekiel called it a "cubit," a standard unit of measure in ancient times. However, Ezekiel's "royal" cubit is sometimes miscalculated, or confused with the common cubit. For the purposes of this study, this tool can be summed as follows:

- It was (and remains) the only *royal* and appropriate measuring device to be employed in laying out the maps and architecture of Messiah's land, city and Temple to come
- It is *not* the common cubit (approximately 18 inches long)

---

[18] Hebrews 4:12; 1 Peter 1:23.

- ☐ It has its precedent, for sacred usage, in the Temple of Solomon
- ☐ It must have an accuracy consistent with the Lord's own demand for precision in measuring devices
- ☐ It has in its pedigree the ancient Egyptian penchant for accuracy
- ☐ It had, for Ezekiel, real and measurable markings

One royal cubit of the Bible equates approximately with:

- ☐ 20.64 inches / 524 millimeters
- ☐ 1.72 feet / 0.52 meters
- ☐ 0.00036 miles / 0.0005 kilometers

Since the same measuring device is used for large regions, smaller areas, individual buildings, and even architectural details, it will be very handy to have these values in mind, and carry this important tool in our luggage.

Qualified Guides

Though we've seen some dangers, we have our defenses and our main weapon; and we have our vital map. But if we needed to discuss a final means of preparation, surely it would be under the heading of guidance.

First and foremost, we must seek the Holy Spirit of God, humbly and earnestly, for understanding along the way. Though this study may appear to be a finished and conclusive teaching, it is not; and His guidance is vital. There will be areas where, based solely upon the Biblical evidence, entire books could be written – but here are treated only briefly. Most importantly, only the Lord knows what you must do with the information He grants you by His Word. For all these things, we need the help of His Spirit.

In addition, it would be helpful to have some flesh-and-blood human beings that know the way; a living and breathing guide or two, actual people who have trod these paths in advance and who can give us practical advice. As it turns out, we do indeed have such living guides. And our preparations would not be complete without appreciating them a little more personally. Since their words were recorded thousands of years ago, it would be easy to think these men long dead. Not so! Enoch, for example, perhaps the very first prophet, never experienced death but instead was bodily taken away to Heaven[19]. Abraham,

[19] Genesis 5:24, with Jude 14 and Hebrews 11:5.

another original prophet[20] and father in faith to us all[21], "*was looking forward to the city with foundations, whose architect and builder is God*[22]." As to that man's living status, Jesus Himself said very clearly that Abraham *is still alive*[23]. These are just two examples of human beings that saw God's land in Heaven, yet are still alive (there), with (obviously) multitudes of other faithful ones.

Included in those multitudes are certain prophets who physically experienced Messiah's future dominion, even though they walked this earth long ago. So as we utilize the details and instructions they recorded, it is important to understand that they and their words are not desiccated and irrelevant. Instead:

- Their guidance, though penned by them or uttered through them, has its origin in the Lord: *His* Word never perishes[24], and is itself alive[25]; thus their words still speak.

- Their voices, though conveyed by the body they had on earth, still resonate from and in Heaven – where these men yet live, walk and speak, even now.

- Their data, though recorded two or three millennia ago, or more, are not dimmed by the passage of time: for a thousand years to us are but a day in God's eyes[26].

True, sometimes their guidance is enigmatic, even cryptic. This is because the Lord Himself has decided to ensure that certain passages *are* puzzling:

> *He said, "Listen to my words: "When a prophet of the LORD is among you, I reveal myself to him in* **visions**, *I speak to him in* **dreams**. *7 But this is not true of my servant Moses; he is faithful in all my house. 8 With him I speak face to face, clearly and not* **in riddles**...
> *Numbers 12:6-8b, NIV*

---

[20] Though Enoch was eventually understood to have been a prophet (Jude 14), Abraham was the first person to be declared in the Bible as a prophet of the Lord (Genesis 20:7).
[21] Romans 4:16.
[22] Hebrews 11:10, NIV.
[23] See Matthew 22:31-32, Mark 12:26-27, Luke 20:37-38 for this clear point. See also Luke 16:22-31 for an example of Abraham's activity in Heaven.
[24] Isaiah 40:8, 55:11; Matthew 24:35, Mark 13:31, Luke 21:33; 1 Peter 1:25.
[25] Romans 1:16; Hebrews 4:12; 1 Peter 1:23.
[26] Psalms 90:4; quoted in 2 Peter 3:8.

Yet as the times draw nearer for those affected, the Lord makes His "riddles" clearer for them[27]. So for whatever puzzles He has given us by way of His prophets, to the extent it pleases Him in *our* day, we have those same living prophets to help us. That is, we have their carefully-chosen words, awaiting our attention, with the assistance of the Holy Spirit.

We also have, as mentioned earlier, their experiential knowledge of the things we are after. With certain passages, to us, it's a chapter in the Bible. For the prophet involved, it was being pushed forward in time, and literally seeing and touching and otherwise sensing things in a far distant future. With certain passages, it is important to understand that the prophet was actually there, *in advance*. Like professional photographers, caught in sometimes dangerous settings, and shooting from different camera angles, they saw what they saw and wrote in accordance with God's purposes.

From differing times, paths and perspectives, these men are our forward scouts. The Lord brought them to a future place, brought them back home, and commanded them to instruct us in accordance with His will.

Clearly, spiritual purposes and lessons abound at every turn of the prophecies, for God's Word is, like a diamond, multi-faceted in how it sheds His Light. Even so, we must not overlook the reality of what was observed by these scouts, nor diminish the factuality of the details given. These were real men when they walked the earth, every bit as real as you or I. For the times when they walked the future earth, we should respect what they reported.

Such people will be our guides, by way of God's Word. They are trustworthy, for they lived their daily lives in accordance with God's commands. And they paid a heavy price[28] to convey to us what they did. These prophets are adequate as instructors, for they have journeyed already to this region ahead of us. And they were personally and heavily motivated in the accuracy of their messages, to that we might be better prepared[29].

---

[27] E.g., Daniel 8:26, 12:4, 12:8-9; contrast Revelation 22:10 for the opposite effect.
[28] E.g., Hebrews 12.
[29] For more on the personal passion for accuracy felt by our main prophetic "guide" here, please see Appendix B: Ezekiel's Witness.

Awaiting Riches

There are, of course, reasons for this expedition: rewards to be found along the way, and at the journey's end.

Treasure #1: A Better Glimpse of Heaven

The "land" of Heaven is one of the biggest and deepest hopes we have. It is the homeland of our God; and until He creates something even better[30], Heaven remains our ultimate Promised Land. The object of our exploration, the earthly land of Messiah to come, is very similar for it will represent the Heavenly dominion within our present creation. If we can learn something about the latter, we can learn something about Heaven as well.

Here's an example. Hard Biblical information on Heaven's City is hard to come by. Yet the Lord *does* grant us a *huge* amount of practical detail[31] on an earthly city on the horizon: that in which He, as King of all earthly kings, will personally dwell, in *this* world and realm. Though the Millennial City proper is not the focus here, the same principle applies to the land as a whole: that in studying the country of Israel in Messiah's day, we can better appreciate the reality and wonder of God's "country"[32] in Heaven.

Treasure #2: A Better Glimpse of the Bigger Picture

Again, Messiah's country on the horizon has amazing coverage in Scripture, while its heavenly counterpart does not. For example, one doesn't see in the Bible much information on heavenly transportation, geographic division, or human industry. But one does notice such things for the Millennial Holy Land. This contrast is striking; and surely it must have a purpose.

The premise here is that the Bible as a whole demonstrates God's program for His creation, and its prophecies emphasize what is next on His timeline for it.

---

[30] Revelation 21:1-22:5.

[31] As will be seen, these details are first indicated by Moses (in the *Torah*, or "Pentateuch"), spread amongst the prophetic books, echoed throughout the Psalms, and confirmed in the New Testament – with special clarifications contained in the book of Revelation.

[32] See Hebrews 11:13-16, where Heaven is described as a "country" superior to any on Earth.

Indeed, Messiah's coming land declares God's fulfilled promises for this creation. Further, since the wonders of Heaven will give way to something eternal and earthier[33], Messiah's country announces that final and eternal environment where God rules directly over humankind. So in studying this next big section of God's timeline for this Earth, we are reminded of God's overarching program, and of where we stand on His timeline.

Now, in full disclosure, I owe it to you to convey what my understanding of "God's Program" is.

- That there is only one God who created everything, and who "dwells" in a super-natural realm known as Heaven – even though that environment cannot contain Him, let alone an earthly Temple (1 Kings 8:27; 2 Chronicles 2:6).

- That God's purpose in creating us in the first place is to have an eternal and loving relationship with beings having His likeness, a spirit breathed in from His own, and a nature imbued with His; and that we *choose* to return a heart-love in *reliance* upon Him (from Genesis 1:26, to David's psalms, to John 3:16, to Revelation 22:21, and all points in between).

- That God is utterly holy, and we are not; yet He has been moving throughout history to accomplish His objectives, bridging the holiness-chasm by becoming our sacrificial Lamb, thereby bringing His holiness to us.

- That God's main program of obtaining us, as a people in eternal covenant with Him, began with Abraham; and that in faith, like that man[34], we trust in His provision for our faith and cleansing; that His program further proceeded with Abraham's offspring, to Jacob-Israel, and his descendants.

- That God's promises to Israel – both the people and the land –are incomplete; yet the promises are firm, and must be fulfilled[35].

- That a brief period generally referred to as "The Tribulation" will transpire between the age we live in now, and that of the Lord's reign on Earth.

---

[33] As in the new and conjoined Heaven-Earth of Revelation 21-22.

[34] As with Abram, even before he was renamed Abraham: Genesis 15:6; quoted in Romans 4:3, Galatians 3:6, James 2:23.

[35] See Romans 11, for example.

And here is where this study comes into play:

- That while God's heavenly Country is that to which Abraham looked[36], its emblem – the Millennial Kingdom – will be established in this current earthly realm; that in this coming time, His promises to Abraham and Israel will be entirely completed.

- That in this period to come, Messiah will bring healing to all creation, reversing all despoiling by the Enemy since the original Curse was levied.

- That after this lengthy Messianic era or "day," and after all historical promises of God have found their resolution, the heavenly and earthly dominions will be made one, in an unprecedented union between the natural and supernatural[37].

Though our opinions of God's overarching plan will vary, we should be able to agree that His Word speaks often and strongly of His Anointed returning to Earth as King of kings. If recent history is any indication, we can perhaps also sense that this coming may be soon. It is refreshing to be reminded that wonderful things – such as the land of our study – are just around the bend. Through good times or bad, we can treasure the knowledge that our Savior has the victory, and that He is in control of the greater story.

Treasure #3: Hope and Strength

If Messiah is coming soon, the precursive times will get disturbing indeed. Especially for the countless number of believers that will experience those events[38], a study of the "silver lining" behind the dark clouds is called for. And even if you or I do not participate in those foretold activities to come, we can still gain hope from the knowledge of impending victory of our Lord.

So what we want to do here is get at the truth of the matter, what lies on the other side of the "tribulation." As we focus on such outcomes, we see that what the Lord is doing in these transitional times is all good news for those that

---

[36] Compare Hebrews 11:13-16 with 11:8-10, 12:22, 13:14.

[37] As seen in Revelation 21-22.

[38] The number of believers that die during the "Tribulation" are said to be "without number" (Revelation 7:9-17). However, a comparable population apparently survives until the Lord's Coming (1 Thessalonians 4:15-17). Together, this is an enormous body of people.

put their faith in Him[39]. As we keep seeking out God's purposes in this coming transition of ages, and say No to fear-strategies of the Enemy, we will gradually get stronger, more resilient, and increasingly effective toward our Lord's agenda – in spite of circumstances.

In many areas of life, the places where we're least prepared for action are where the threats seem so distant that they seem non-issues. But if the "battle" comes to one's doorstep, as it were, it certainly gets attention. Likewise, as events related to the "end times" proceed, certain commanded activities will become non-optional. Loving one's neighbor, taking prayer seriously, not being a glutton, etc., are examples. But before times get tough, we can voluntarily study the Lord's agenda, and be motivated towards greater faith and obedience, bringing further strengthening.

Though the study before us is just one aspect of the Kingdom on the horizon, there is much encouragement. With God's guidance, it encourages us toward greater perspective, hope and motivation, leading to an increased inner strength that cannot be easily shaken.

Treasure #4: A Cohesive People

Ultimately, God will obtain for Himself a human community for all eternity, a "nation" fully unified with Him and one another, a holy Bride "without spot or wrinkle"[40]. Though this eternal people began with the offspring of Abraham, Isaac and (specifically) Jacob-Israel, it will ultimately consist of every human nationality[41].

Contrast that thought with how things are now. It is hard to imagine Christians being unified, let alone Jews *and* Christians – under one faith in the same Messiah. Yet for all eternity, as the Bible shows, it will be so[42]. How will this unity come about?

Between now and that point of cohesion, there is a prophesied period that is without precedent in history. The closest comparison is when David and Solomon ruled over Israel, with Solomon's dominion becoming even greater than David's[43]. Israel will once again have a King, as will all the world: the returning Son of David, even greater than Solomon[44], will reign from His throne in Jerusalem. He will not rule over that land only, but over all the nations of the

---

[39] E.g., Deuteronomy 8:2-5, 16-17; Psalms 46:1-2; Jeremiah 24:6-7; Romans 8:28.

[40] Ephesians 5:26-27.

[41] Presaged in Genesis 18:18, dramatically evidenced in Revelation 5:9, and taught in innumerable points in between.

[42] E.g., Ephesians 2:11-22.

[43] 1 Kings 1:37.

[44] Matthew 12:42; Luke 11:31

world[45] as King of all kings. Under His rule, unity will prevail for a thousand years – a millennium[46].

Even now, this is a substantial treasure in understanding for us. The "millennial" era, under the rule of Lord Yeshua, will see the great disparities between God's people resolved, with peace brought to every nation on this planet. Before the ultimate setting of the Eternal City[47] arrives, this coming (and final) age of this Earth will demonstrate unity amongst all God's children. If foreknowledge has value, this understanding is very valuable indeed. As we explore the land of the coming King, we will get to know better the "central" land of the world, the place that all the faithful will long to go to:

> *This is what the Lord Almighty says: "In those days ten men from all languages and nations will take firm hold of one Jew by the hem of his robe and say, 'Let us go with you, because we have heard that God is with you.' "*
> *Zechariah 8:23, NIV*

As we proceed into any study of "those days" ahead, we get more familiar with God's plan for a cohesive people. During our expedition, the reality of that unified people will be striking, perhaps giving you and me a better sense of our bigger eternal family. And who knows? Perhaps the Lord will show us how to implement more of that unity in the here-and-now.

The Compelling Mission

Should we be encouraged to probe these matters of Messiah's Kingdom? Do we even have God's blessing to do so? The answer is an emphatic Yes!

One discouraging factor should be flipped around immediately. Claims about "the end times" and the "end of the world" have come and gone over the decades and centuries. There have been plenty of such false claims; and there will be plenty more[48]. But instead of being dispirited by such things, we can and should turn the argument around, for the steadily growing drumbeat of false alarms and false prophets *confirms* what Jesus predicted:

> *And then if any man shall say to you, Lo, here is Christ; or, lo, he is there; believe him not: 22 For false Christs and false prophets shall rise, and shall shew signs and*

[45] E.g., Psalms 2:7-12; Revelation 12:5.
[46] Revelation 20:6-7.
[47] E.g., Revelation 21-22.
[48] Matthew 24:23-24; Mark 13:21-22.

wonders, to seduce, if it were possible, even the elect. 23 But take ye heed: behold, I have foretold you all things.
Mark 13:21-23, KJV

Another issue might nag some folks: do we really have permission to make this journey? Yes! For the Lord makes it clear that though certain things remain undisclosed by Him (such as the details of Heaven, Hell and eternity forward), the subjects He *has* elaborated upon in Scripture "*belong to us and our children forever*[49]." Moreover,

All scripture is given by inspiration of God, and is profitable for doctrine, for reproof, for correction, for instruction in righteousness: 17 That the man of God may be perfect, thoroughly furnished unto all good works.
2 Timothy 3:16-17, KJV

All of God's Word should be studied by us who depend it, including the sections pertaining to Messiah's coming land, for these also are passages able to instruct and be "*furnished unto all good works.*" Even more so for those approaching the transition into that age. Indeed, *if* we are sensing that society is increasingly rejecting God, *if* we are hearing more false teachings about the "end of the world," *if* we are discouraged because it all seems like the bad guys are in charge, then this is the time to remind ourselves of our Lord's coming victory. This is the time to avail ourselves of the truth He has given us, to see what His Word is revealing in our times.

In addition to these points, a simple fact remains: we are all commanded to be alert to our King's coming. Books abound on the "tribulation," but it is His actual arrival that we are to be especially anticipating:

"Therefore ***keep watch****, because you do not know on* ***what day your Lord will come****."*
Matthew 24:42, NIV

"Even so, when you see these things happening, you know that it is near, right at the door… 33 ***Be on guard! Be alert!*** *You do not know when that time will come."*
Mark 13:29,33, NIV

"Be always on the watch*, and pray that you may be able to escape all that is about to happen, and* ***that you may be able to stand before the Son of Man."***
Luke 21:36, NIV

---

[49] Deuteronomy 29:29.

> *Therefore you do not lack any spiritual gift* **as you eagerly wait for our Lord Jesus Christ to be revealed.** *8 He will keep you strong to the end, so that you will be blameless on the day of our Lord Jesus Christ.*
> *1 Corinthians 1:7-8, NIV*

> *But our citizenship is in heaven. And* **we eagerly await a Savior** *from there, the Lord Jesus Christ…*
> *Philippians 3:20, NIV*

> *…while* **we wait for the blessed hope** *— the* **glorious appearing** *of our great God and Savior, Jesus Christ…*
> *Titus 2:13, NIV*

> *Therefore, prepare your minds for action; be self-controlled;* **set your hope fully** *on the grace to be given you* **when Jesus Christ is revealed.**
> *1 Peter 1:13, NIV*

> ***"Behold, I am coming soon! Blessed is he who keeps the words of the prophecy in this book."***
> *Revelation 22:7, NIV*

How better to honor the King than by an alertness to His coming? We cannot lay palm fronds across His path, at least not right now[50]. But we can look toward the same events as He, and study His dominion. In the case of this study, we will explore one key aspect: the geography of that Kingdom.[51]

And so, we begin. Like the spies sent out to explore the original Promised Land of the Exodus, we seek to map its final counterpart, the Promised Land of Messiah's Kingdom, the realm of the returning Son of David.

---

[50] Compare Revelation 7:9 with John 12:13.

[51] Though Messiah will be King of all kings of the world (e.g., 1 Timothy 6:15; Revelation 7:14, 19:16), he will be the "direct" ruler of Israel in His day. So while the whole Earth will be His dominion, we will be drawing special attention in this study to His "natural" country ruled by His "father" David.

Chapter 2: Border Reconnaissance

"... When you enter Canaan, the land that will be allotted to you as an inheritance will have these boundaries..."

Numbers 34:2B, NIV

Because I swore with uplifted hand to give it to your forefathers, this land will become your inheritance.

Ezekiel 47:14, NIV

You showed favor to your land, O Lord; you restored the fortunes of Jacob.

Psalms 85:1, NIV

Entering the Land

Of all the geographic regions of the Earth, it is the land of Israel that is repeatedly described in the Bible as being special to the Creator. It is from this unique territory that the Lord chose long ago to enact His main interventions upon this world. It is the region that Abraham explored at God's direction, and was permanently promised to him by way of his descendants of both faith[52] and blood.

This is the "promised land," so named because it is guaranteed to God's people via His promises to Abraham, a promise confirmed to and through his son Isaac and his grandson Jacob-Israel. From those patriarchs forward, the Bible proclaims a promise that, ultimately[53], the land and the people will together be safe and prosperous.

Some day in the future, Messiah will fulfill this great story, weaving together the many threads and layers of promise associated with this region. Bringing blessing upon Israel and all His creation, reigning from Jerusalem, the King will demonstrate God's faithfulness to His Word and His people. Such is the divine and prophesied import of this section of the Earth's surface. We now enter this very territory, not as it is now, but as it is prophesied to be: the Holy Land in its glory, in the coming Day of the Lord's reign.

The Holy Land in Messiah's coming day is not defined by current geo-political boundaries, but by specific promises of God through His prophets. Our first task will be to understand what those markers are, doing our best to correlate them with present geography and generally survey what the borders will be.

The prophet Ezekiel will be our primary guide here. The Lord Himself dictated to Ezekiel these distinct boundaries of Israel, in the time frame to which this man was briefly transported[54]. In fact, these are borders that God Almighty *swore* to preserve and enforce for that time, harking back to those boundaries promised to Abraham[55], generally confirming those given by Moses[56].

What follows is a brief point-by-point walk-through[57] of these boundaries given by Ezekiel and commented upon by me. On the surface, these details may

---

52 Romans 4.

53 That is, even in spite of prior dispersions of His first-chosen people (see, for example, Leviticus 26:33-46, Ezekiel 47:14).

54 Ezekiel 47:13-21, 48:1-8, 48:22-29.

55 Ezekiel 47:14b.

56 See Numbers 34.

57 For a more in-depth discussion: Beitzel, Barry J. "As the Land Prepared By God." The Moody Atlas of Bible Lands, Chicago, IL, Moody Publishers, Inc, 2000.

seem dry and irrelevant. But be assured: as we hike this route, we are connecting future events with declarations ancient and unchanging. We are participating in the foreseeing, affirming it to be a living prophecy.

Initial Mapping: The Northern Border

We will follow Ezekiel and begin with the most difficult to interpret: the northern border. We will take it in steps, and you can follow along in your own Bible.

The northern border (47:15-17, KJV):

[1] *And this shall be the border of the land toward the north side, from the Great Sea…* (47:15) This northwest position on the Mediterranean coast is the beginning and ending point of the boundary we are about to tour.

[2] *… the way of Hethlon…* (47:15; cf 48:1) In Bible commentaries, Hethlon's location is usually associated with "modern Heitela." Unfortunately, it is hard to find evidence of such a village, modern or otherwise. But whatever its present name is, Heitela-Hethlon was located on the el-Kabir river, with the "Hethlon road" (or "way") coinciding with the Eleutherus valley[58]. This east-west valley forms the border between Lebanon and Syria in this area.

[3] *… as men go to Zedad…* (47:15) Fortunately, we can identify the "Hethlon road" by a more solid means. It was used to travel from the coast to Zedad (modern Sadad) and other points inland (as cited in verse 16 and also 48:1). The Eleutherus valley is the obvious place for such a road, cutting eastward through the northern Lebanon Mountains on the way to this ancient city which remains to this day.

[4] *Hamath…* (47:15) Though ancient Lebweh has been traditionally selected for this site, others point out that the Hebrew word "lebo" (in 48:1) may likely mean "entrance to" or "going toward" the Hamath area[59]. Moving along our border then, one encounters this valley that slopes down (and north) to Hamath.

---

[58] Cf the ISBE, topic of "Hethlon."

[59] Every instance of the phrase "Lebo Hamath" in the NIV Study Bible is footnoted with such a caveat. Furthermore, the "lebo" of verse 15 appears to modify Zedad ("as going to"), which is why the KJV renders it as shown in step 3 (the word "men" isn't in the Hebrew though).

[5] … *Berothah,* … (47:16) The location is unknown, but the modern town of Bereitan is often favored, with an alternate being Wadi Brissa[60]. Both are quite southward from our path, with Wadi Brissa even backtracking. Regardless, our trek takes us eastward to Zedad, past either a to-be-determined location for Berothah, or a road that went to it[61].

[6] … *Sibraim, which is between the border of Damascus and the border of Hamath;* … (47:16) Opinions vary for Sibraim, but it may correlate with Ziphron, Khirbet Sanbariyeh, or some other place yet to be unearthed. It stood between the ancient lands of Hamath (to the north) and Damascus (to the south).

[7] … *Hazer Hatticon, which is by the coast of Hauran.* (47:16) Though the location is not known, it was situated somewhere along the border ("coast") of Hauran. Like Damascus and Hamath, "Hauran" refers to the larger region dominated by that city. The Hauran district, centered on Mt Hauran, was to the southeast of Damascus.

[8] *And the border from the sea…* (47:17) Verse 17 is a recap of the northern border, but going in the opposite direction.

[9] … *shall be Hazar Enan…* (47:17; cf 48:1) We now have a restatement of the end point, citing a specific town[62]. Meaning "village of a spring," this locale is generally agreed to be modern Al Qaryateen and its oasis.

[10] … *the border of Damascus…* (47:17; cf 48:1) Confirmation that our border lies to the north of the ancient district of Damascus.

[11] … *and the north northward, and the border of Hamath.* (47:17; cf 48:1) Again, a confirmation that our border lies to the south of the ancient district of Hamath.

[12] *And this is the north side.* (47:17)

---

[60] E.g., per ISBE, topic of "Berothah": "Its site is unknown. Ewald connected it with Beirut… but Ezekiel's description excludes this view. Others have sought it in the Wady Brissa, in the East slope of Lebanon, North of Baalbec. A more plausible conjecture identifies it with Bereitan (Brithen), a village somewhat South of Baalbec…"

[61] The "lebo" of verse 15 may perhaps apply to all four cities named, e.g., "…as men go to Zedad, Hamath, Berothah, Sibraim…" In other words, this "Hethlon Road" was used to travel to all those destinations, but did not necessarily pass directly through them.

[62] Per the NJPS, Hazar Enan is "apparently identical with Hazer-hatticon in v. 16."

The figure below[63] looks back on the steps we've just taken, with the "Suggested Border" being a smoothed-out depiction (the actual border may well follow major features of the future terrain, when it comes down to it). The "Alternate Border" (here and in two following maps) is included for further reference, should you wish to compare notes with a recognized authority on Biblical mapping.[64]

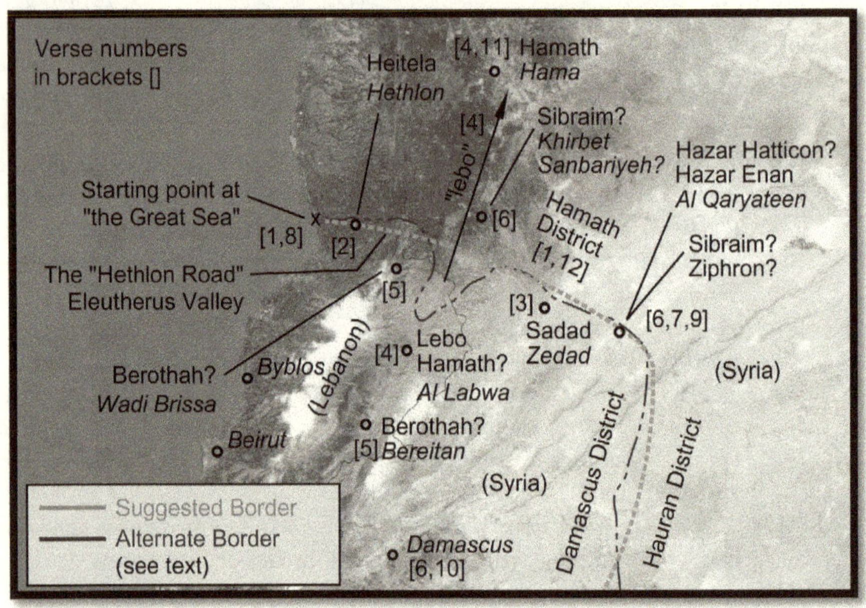

Figure 1: Ezekiel's Northern Border

Though some markers can be firmly ascertained, others cannot. And though most instructions are straightforward, some terms (like "lebo") remain puzzling. Fortunately, exactitude isn't what we're after in this investigation, only a basic grasp of this northern border segment in the era to come. What we have then is an essentially east-west border from a point north of Tripoli, along the al-Kabir river in the Eleutherus valley, past the high plains opening upon Hama to the north (and Bereitan to the south), through (or near) Sibraim (location TBD), through (or near) Sadad, and ending at al-Qaryateen.

---

[63] Background images of all maps in this chapter are from the NASA satellite image file "Middle East," February 17 2003, Jacques Descloitres, MODIS Rapid Response Team, NASA/GSFC, 4 January 2008, <http://visibleearth.nasa.gov/view.php?id=65114>. Color / higher-resolution versions are available for download at www.EarthAwaits.com.

[64] Beitzel, Barry J. The Moody Atlas of Bible Lands, Chicago, IL, Moody Publishers, Inc, 2000. Tracings here by permission.

At the time of this writing at least, a digital form of access is about the only way a non-resident can journey here. It is a region hugely in conflict[65], rendering a literal trip practically impossible. A "fly through" via Google Earth[66], however, allows us to virtually hike this border and get a sense of the terrain, towns, and other features. Whether you choose to do such a virtual trip or not, this northern arc of the prophesied border passes through lands that are clearly outside of contemporary Israel. In fact, it takes in Lebanon entirely – making this information from our prophet-guide Ezekiel highly controversial.

But let us fast forward to the time of Messiah's dominion, when the entire world will enjoy His reign of peace. During His reign, below this northern arc will be the country of His direct jurisdiction; above it will be another country – presumably Syria, or some other national entity derived from ancient Assyria[67]. To the south will be the renewed Holy Land, specifically the tribal province[68] of Dan[69] – whose name means "*[God] has vindicated [me]*[70]." But on both sides of the border, *all* will benefit from the King's wisdom and justice. And on both sides, in what is now a scarred, war-torn, and often barren landscape, creation will flourish mightily.

A couple of technical points are worth noting, applying to all segments of the border. Geography in the region will *not* be perfectly identical to what it is right now, due to major tectonic events in the Tribulation. However, Sadad, the "Hethlon road," and other features will still be recognizable in the Millennial era – otherwise, the prophecy's fulfillment would be impossible to verify. One way or another, perhaps by future archeology (even in the Millennial era), the Lord will confirm what He declared to Ezekiel.

Initial Mapping: The Eastern Border

While the northern boundary is mainly located by specific towns, the eastern one is mostly described by edges of regions, presenting challenges of a different sort. Though we are only talking about one verse (47:18), translations differ quite a bit. See for yourself how differently scholars have rendered it:

---

[65] For example, with the Syrian civil war, Homs (located near our prophesied border), Al-Qaryateen and other nearby cities have been especially afflicted in 2011 and thereafter.

[66]See <http://www.google.com/earth>.

[67] Ancient Assyria will again play a role, during Messiah's kingdom: Isaiah 19:23-25.

[68] Though the Bible does not use the term "province," words such as "state" or "county" seem inadequate or misleading. In referring to all these cartographic strips of land that Ezekiel defines, the author has therefore elected to employ the term "province."

[69] Ezekiel 48:1-2.

[70] Genesis 30:6.

NASB: And the east side, from between Hauran, Damascus, Gilead, and the land of Israel, shall be the Jordan; from the north border to the eastern sea you shall measure. This is the east side.

NIV: On the east side the boundary will run between Hauran and Damascus, along the Jordan between Gilead and the land of Israel, to the eastern sea and as far as Tamar. This will be the east boundary.

NJPS: As the eastern limit: a line between Hauran and Damascus, and between Gilead and the land of Israel: with the Jordan as a boundary, you shall measure down to the Eastern Sea. That shall be the eastern limit.

LXX[71]*: And the places toward the east between Hauran, and between Damascus, and between Gilead, and between the land of Israel, the Jordan separates unto the sea the one towards the east of Palm-grove; these are the borders towards the east.*

KJV: And the east side ye shall measure from Hauran, and from Damascus, and from Gilead, and from the land of Israel by Jordan, from the border unto the east sea. And this is the east side.

So where does the eastern border run? For our purposes, it depends on the translation one might favor, where one places the districts named, punctuation used, whether one tries to blend in Numbers 34 in the process, and how the translators rendered the Hebrew word *beyn* (usually meaning "between," but sometimes "from [out of]"). The task is not hopeless though, because we can be reasonably confident about a few geographic things.

- The district of Damascus is already contained within our border, southward of the northern segment just surveyed.

- Our eastern-most point of the northern border has already been described as being on Hauran's border (with Hauran, as argued, lying eastward).

- We see here in verse 18 again that the districts of Damascus (to the west) and Hauran (to the east) were adjacent one another, and that we are to follow this roughly north-south line from where we left off.

---

71 Charles Van der Pool ed.,The Greek Septuagint, as translated in The Apostolic Bible, 16 Dec 2007, <www.apostolicbible.com>.

- □ Though the KJV translates the term *beyn* as coming "from" these districts, the word is elsewhere in Ezekiel consistently employed in the sense of "between." So "between" it will be.

- □ Mt. Hauran, contained within the ancient district of Hauran, lies southeast of Damascus. To steer between those districts, the border (as it goes southward) must start swinging westward.

- □ Such a westward swing is also required if the Jordan is to become part of the boundary as we continue southward.

- □ At that lower point, the ancient region of Gilead lies to the east of the Jordan, and our border.

So, now to the "map" of Scripture. Again, the numbered steps refer to locations on the figure that follows.

The eastern border (47:18, NIV):

[13] *On the east side the boundary will run…* We begin where we left off, from a village northeast of Damascus, Al Qaryateen. We will be moving southward, facing in that direction.

[14] … *between Hauran and Damascus…* As we face southward, with the ancient district of Damascus on our right (to the west), we are gradually see Mount Hauran on our left (to the east). Our path is now heading southwest, then almost due west as we head to the next feature.

[15] *…along the Jordan…* Alongside the Jordan River, the border now travels south, with that river as the continuing demarcation line.

[16] *…between Gilead and the land of Israel,* To the west is the land of Israel, with ancient Gilead to the east. By following the Jordan the border is easily identifiable.

[17] *…to the eastern sea…* We follow that river all the way down to the Dead Sea.

[18] *…and as far as Tamar.* Following the Septuagint, the NIV adds this note. Since it is absent in the Hebrew, other translations do not. We will deal with Tamar in the discussion of the southern border, where it appears as the starting point for that segment.

[19] *This will be the east boundary.*

For this eastern border, the findings here generally agree with those of others [72] -- with the differences revolving around whether Mt. Hauran is contained within the future Holy Land, or (the position here) to the east of its northern border. Be that as it may, Mt. Hauran, like all other mountains, will be subject to the Lord's Mountain: for Mount Zion will be "chief among the mountains" in the "last days[73]."

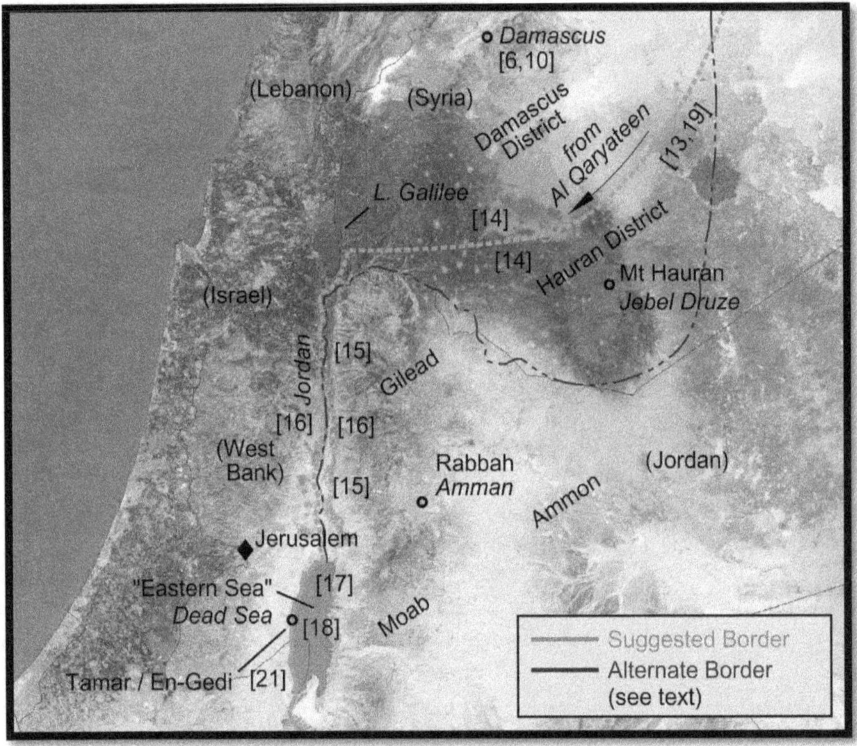

Figure 2: Ezekiel's Eastern Border

The thing that stands out for this border segment is its odd "P" shape, due starting out far to the east up north, but moving westward to the Jordan in the south. We will return to this issue soon. But for now, let's recognize the peculiar contour for what it is.

---

[72] E.g., Beitzel. See also Schmitt, John W. & Laney, J. Carl. Messiah's Coming Temple, Grand Rapids, MI, Kregel Publications, 1997, p125.

[72] Cf the ISBE, topic of "Hethlon."

[73] Isaiah 2:2; Micah 4:1.

Initial Mapping: The Southern Border

From this point forward, things get slightly easier. The southern leg is described in 47:19, beginning with a location called Tamar:

> *On the south side it will run from* ***Tamar*** *as far as the waters of Meribah Kadesh, then along the Wadi [of Egypt] to the Great Sea. This will be the south boundary.*

Each of these border segments has at least one big issue, and Tamar is the one here. Tamar means "palm tree[74]," and a couple of women in the Bible have been given that name. As a place name though[75], we have only a handful of references. Keeping in mind that a "row" or "grove" of palm trees would be called *hazazon tamar*, or *Chatsetsown Tamar*[76], we observe the following:

> *And they returned, and came to En-mishpat, which is Kadesh, and smote all the country of the Amalekites, and also the Amorites that dwelt in* ***Hazezon-tamar****.*
> *Genesis 14:7, KJV*

> *...and, behold, they be* ***Hazazon-tamar****, which is En-Gedi.*
> *2 Chronicles 20:2b, KJV*

Per the above, Hazazon-Tamar is strongly associated with Kadesh, just as in 47:19 (though the prophet apparently did not use the "rows" or "grove" prefix of *Chatsetsown*). Further, it is explicitly equated with En-Gedi, a town on the west coast of the Dead Sea. So is the Chronicler's Hazazon-Tamar the same place as Ezekiel's Tamar? The translators of the Septuagint apparently felt so, adding the "grove" term:

> *...the Jordan separates unto the [Dead] sea the one towards the east of Palm-grove [Tamar]; these are the borders towards the east. And these are the borders towards the south and southwest from Teman, and Palm-grove [Tamar] unto the water of Mariboth Kedesh...*
> *Ezekiel 47:18b-19a, LXX*[77]

---

[74] Strong's OT:8558.
[75] Not to be confused with Baal Tamar, a place to the north near Gibeah (Judges 20:33).
[76] Strong's OT:2688.
[77] Charles Van der Pool ed.,The Greek Septuagint, as translated in The Apostolic Bible, 16 Dec 2007, <www.apostolicbible.com>.

Though it might have been helpful if Ezekiel made some mention of groves for Tamar, the ancient translators of the Septuagint apparently felt the connection was obvious. They filled in the blank ("-grove"), for there is no other precedent and candidate location spoken of in the Bible. Therefore, in this last invoking of groves (and "hazazar") for the place name of Tamar, we can see it as the same place spoken of by both the Chronicler and Moses. And though some have disagreed[78], this association simultaneously connects Tamar with En-Gedi, a place we can easily determine a position for. Lying on the west coast of the Dead Sea, En-Gedi retains its name to this day, and is the location of an important nature preserve in Israel.

Having dealt with Tamar, the rest is easy.

The southern border (47:19, NIV):

[20] *On the south side it will run…*The eastern border is established, going down along the Jordan to the Dead Sea.

[21] …*from Tamar*… The border swings around not to the east side of the Dead Sea, but along its western coastline to a point about in the middle of it. We are now at Tamar, a place anciently known for its palm groves, coinciding with the known location of En-Gedi.

[22] … *as far as the waters of Meribah Kadesh*[79]. This place (rendered "waters of strife in Kadesh" in the KJV) is generally considered to be the famous Kadesh-Barnea. The southern border will pass near this place, or at least a wadi or riverbed associated with it.

[23] … *then along the Wadi [of Egypt] to the Great Sea.* This is a significant *wadi*[80], now called Wadi el-Arish. The border simply travels along this natural feature to the Mediterranean Sea.

[24] *This will be the south boundary.*

The following figure plots our steps, indicating alternate opinions for Tamar with a question mark. Wherever Tamar is placed though, the border travels far enough south to encounter Kadesh-Barnea and take the Wadi of Egypt from there.

---

[78] E.g., ISBE, topic of "Tamar," Meaning 2 (William Ewing), where Tamar is placed much further to the south, and connection to 2 Chronicles 20:2 is blatantly dismissed.

[79] For a more in-depth discussion from this point onward: Beitzel, Barry J. "As the Land Prepared By God." The Moody Atlas of Bible Lands, Chicago, IL, Moody Publishers, Inc, 2000.

[80] A *wadi* is a valley or watercourse that, except during periods of rain, remains dry.

Unlike the northern border, this southern one does not extend beyond Israel's current territory. In fact, since it does not even go down to Eilat on the Gulf of Aqaba, the prophesied southern area is actually *less* then at present! However, as we will see, the story of these borders does not quite end with Ezekiel's definitions here.

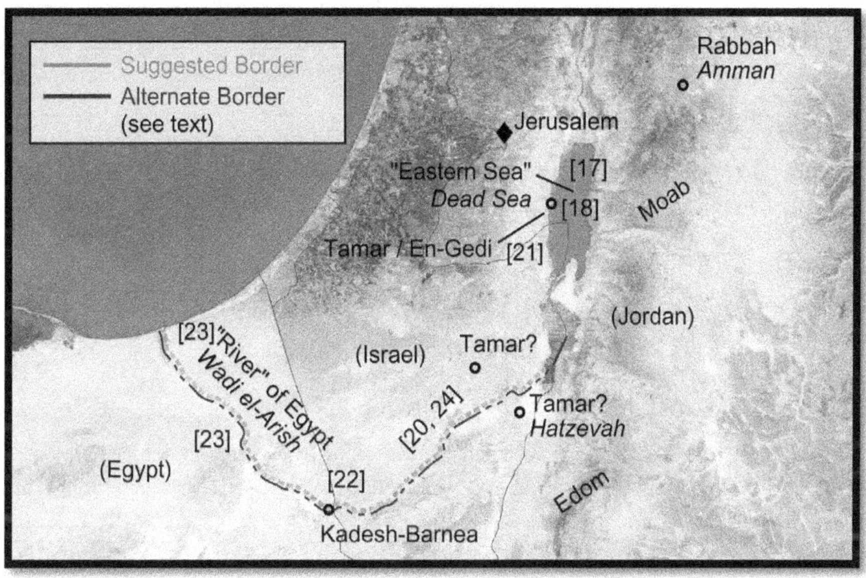

Figure 3: Ezekiel's Southern Border

Instead of Eilat to the south, a new southern tip is indicated for future Israel: Kadesh. This is where the early Israelites camped during much of their wilderness journey, where they complained about water, and where Moses struck the rock from which water broke forth. Hence the term "waters of strife," or "waters of meribah." So it is interesting that, rather than saying that the border simply goes down to Kadesh, it is these waters (and therefore their story), that Ezekiel emphasizes. Perhaps our guide is giving us a hint that there will be a memorial or marker here in Messiah's day, perhaps giving honor to God's undeserved provision to us all – from the very beginning.

Initial Mapping: The Western Border

The last leg is very straightforward.
The western border (all from 47:20, NIV):

[25] *On the west side, the Great Sea will be the boundary*... The western border starts at the southern point where Wadi el-Arish touches the Mediterranean.

[26] ... *to a point opposite Lebo Hamath.* It follows the coast, all the way up to where we began – near the "way to" or "entrance to" the Hamath region.

[27] *This will be the west boundary.*

The Geographic Baseline

We can now step back and look at the Holy Land's overall borders, as specified and promised by the Lord 2.5 millennia ago through Ezekiel. I am using the term "baseline," in the sense that this boundary represents the essential and minimal real estate declared by our guide.

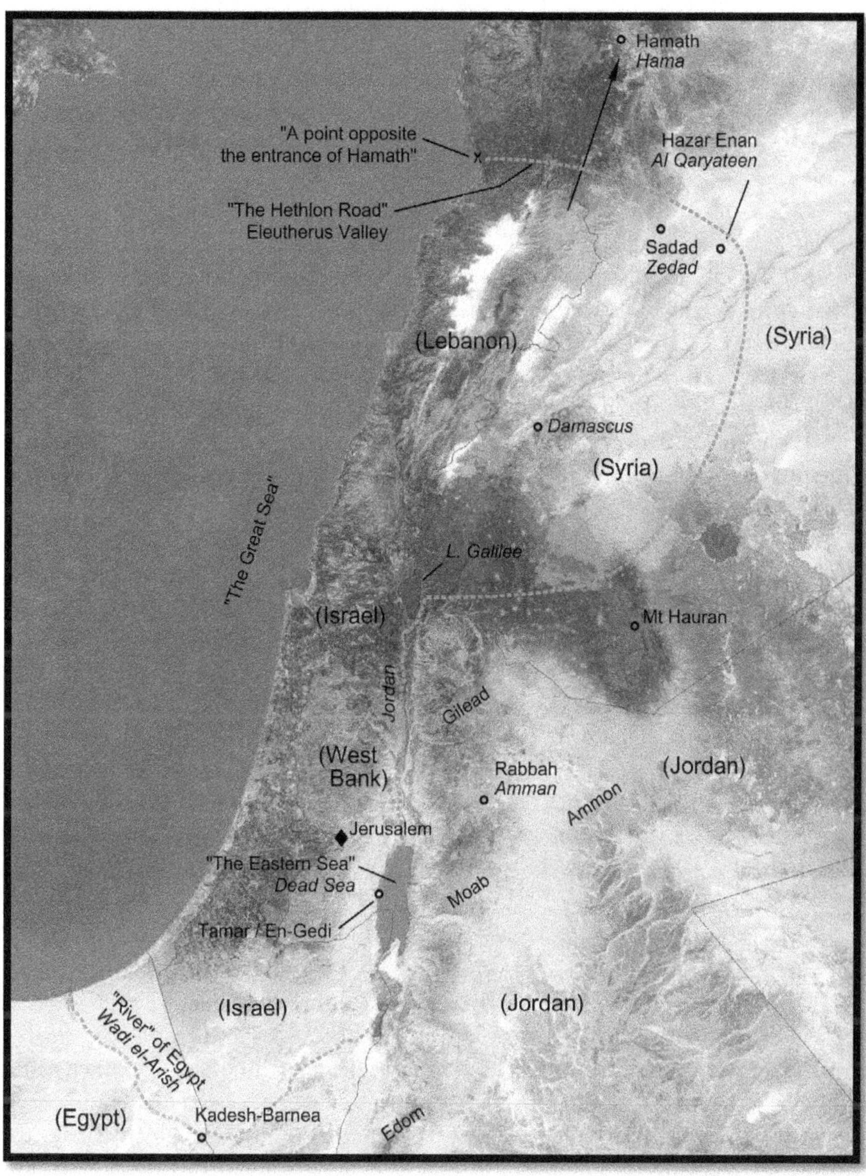

Figure 4: Baseline Borders

This is not, however, the first time the Bible describes the borders we've just walked. Many centuries prior, the practically identical boundary was given through Moses[81] to the original Israelites of the Exodus. Though we will not analyze that passage here, the same key landmarks are present, beginning with the "entrance" to Hamath, east to Zedad, south (though swinging westward) to the Jordan, on down to the Dead Sea, to Kadesh-Barnea, to the coast, and back up north.

Obviously, this is no accident! For what we hear from Ezekiel is nothing less than the firm re-staking out of the land originally promised through Moses.

Of course, God's first-chosen nation was originally intended to fully and permanently occupy this region – and so they eventual did, in the exceptional achievements of David and Solomon. Before and after those two kings though, history tells a different story: for the chosen people did not fully populate the land, nor realize its spatial fullness as their lasting "inheritance."

Even so, the land itself was fully chosen by God. Regardless of dispersion of the people of Israel over history, that land was, and remains, divinely holy and chosen. All of it.

> *"…the land is mine [the Lord's] and you [Israelites] are but aliens and my tenants."*
> *Leviticus 25:23b, NIV*

A big reason for this is that the Lord swore an oath to give this land to Abraham, Isaac and Jacob:

> *This is what the Sovereign Lord says: "These are the boundaries by which you are to divide the land for an inheritance among the twelve tribes of Israel, with two portions for Joseph. 14 You are to divide it equally among them.* ***Because I swore with uplifted hand to give it to your forefathers, this land will become your inheritance.***
> *Ezekiel 47:13-14, NIV*

Though the whole Earth is the Lord's[82], this particular section of it is special to Him, for it is the region in and from which He displays His mighty purposes before the entire world. As it was in ancient times, so it remains: this land belongs to the Lord, modern demography and politics notwithstanding.

And so it will be in the reign of Messiah. For though He will rule the entire world as King of all kings, He will, as a King in His own right, have His own kingdom: the originally-chosen land, inhabited by God's originally-chosen people.

---

[81] Numbers 34:1-12.

[82] Exodus 9:29, 19:5; Deuteronomy 10:14; Job 41:11; Psalms 24:1, 50:12; 1 Corinthians 10:26.

All of this helps explain why these teachings from Ezekiel were expected to get a strong reaction, bringing his contemporaries toward repentance and faith[83]: because in the darkest hour of Babylonian exile, God was declaring that the entire land, as originally, promised would someday be restored to His people. The same message stands to this day, to us: the originally-promised land will be regained, and the Lord's people will inhabit it. What was begun under Yeshua, Moses' aid, will be completed and perfected under Yeshua *ha Mashiach*, Jesus the Anointed.

Other Reactions

Understandably, some folks will not have a positive initial reaction to the baseline map, no matter where it is prophesied in the Bible or by whom. From a current-day political viewpoint, these borders would likely cause concern for peoples other than Israel. For example, the baseline map embraces regions currently occupied by Palestinians[84], all the "West Bank," almost the entire country of Lebanon[85], and a large chunk of Syria. From today's perspective, these peoples, and other nations friendly to them, would perhaps not think fond thoughts of the map presented here.

Such concerns, however, largely miss the point. Recall that we are discussing a geo-political arrangement ordered not by the transient strengths of one people vs. another, but by God Almighty. We are speaking of a condition achieved *not* by Israel's military might, or by that of her allies, but by supernatural interventions of the Lord. This intervention will occur against all human odds, and powers, in a period often referred to as the "end times" or "Jacob's Trouble [tribulation]." So if one doesn't believe in the God of the Bible, none of this should be of concern. But if one does feel alarmed by Him and what He says, wouldn't obediently responding to Him be the logical course of action?

There are folks, perhaps even some Jews or Christians, who might be uncomfortable with the baseline map for other reasons. For example, "fairness" to neighboring nations affected. But let us remember that the God who created all national and ethnic diversity in the first place[86] also designed a fitting territory

---

[83] E.g., Ezekiel 43:10-11.

[84] Note that the term "Palestine" comes from the word "Philistine," and therefore the ancient sea-faring peoples that occupied the eastern coasts of the Mediterranean Sea. Such "sea peoples" were not necessarily of Semitic / Arabic origin; thus the modern term "Palestinian" is somewhat of a misnomer.

[85] Additionally prophesied in Zechariah 10:10.

[86] Genesis 10.

for each people-group[87]. In the day of Messiah's rule, He will resolve and satisfy all such matters of divine national design, ethnic and cultural identity, allocation of natural and geophysical resources, and so forth. In dramatic contrast to all the historic, present and chronic turmoil, the coming Son of David will be the *only* one in earth's history to bring peace to *all* nations[88] in the day of His earthly and majestic reign. He, the Prince of Peace, will undoubtedly provide wondrous and tangible solutions, not only for Israel, but for all peoples.

And for the Lebanese, for example, that find their family homesteads falling within the kingdom of the Prince, would that be so bad? No, the reverse! For as we will see hints of, many special benefits will accrue to citizens of this country on the horizon.

Remaining Puzzles

A remaining reaction to the baseline map, mentioned earlier, is this: why the funny shape? For a region having such import, with that central country being so emblematic of Messiah's reign, and with the Lord already exercising His prerogative to rearrange things in conformity with His purposes[89], why would these borders not be, well, more regular[90]?

One answer is that in the Messianic era, even after "Armageddon," those lands originally granted by God to Israel's ancient "relatives" may still be honored. Thus this strange shape to the land may itself speak to God's faithfulness to His promises: spoken in ancient times to ancient peoples, whose blood will still course in the veins of people yet to come.

But the question is not fully solved with that answer; more levels and issues are involved. For example, keeping in mind God's flexibilities in arranging things in the Reign to come:

[87] E.g., Genesis 10; see also the strict instructions to the Israelites to *not* invade the territories of Edom, Moab and Ammon, due to the fact that the Lord had Himself assigned those lands to those particular people (Deuteronomy 2).

[88] E.g., Isaiah 9:6-7.

[89] E.g., in the very precise sectioning of the land into tribal provinces (to be addressed later).

[90] That is, more in line with the "squareness" of Israel's original encampments in the wilderness, Ezekiel's measurements of the Sacred District, the eternal City of Revelation 21-22, etc.

- ☐ With all the strict east-west and (implicit) rectilinear arrangement in the tribal boundaries[91] (which we will discuss later), why is such a seemingly disorderly boundary laid down for the eastern side?

- ☐ If the northernmost tribes[92] are to be bulged out to the east as far as Al Qaryateen (an extent unprecedented in history), why would not the other tribal provinces be so extended?

- ☐ If Jerusalem is to be the capital city, why is it so non-centered within these described borders? Why would it reside practically *on* the eastern border, up against another country?

- ☐ Since the Jordan River was more centrally located in ancient "original" Israel (that is, when the east bank region was given to the two-and-a-half eastern tribes, under Moses), why would that river here form an eastern extremity in the southern portion of the country (again, in great contrast with the eastward extension of the northern tribes)?

- ☐ To that point, what happens with those eastern tribal lands of Reuben, Gad, and the half-tribe of Manasseh?[93] In the times of Messiah, will Israel give up those ancient holdings?

- ☐ And what about the larger realms conquered and controlled by King David and King Solomon? Do those territories have any bearing, in regards to Messiah's dominion?

Such questions invite the next step in exploring the boundaries of Messiah's country: expansions *beyond* the prophesied baseline map.

---

[91] Ezekiel 48:1-8, 23-28.
[92] Dan, Asher and Naphtali.
[93] Numbers 34:14, etc.

Chapter 3: Certain Expansions

"...and I will settle you after your old estates, and will do better unto you than at your beginnings..."

Ezekiel 36:11b, KJV

"Instead of their shame my people will receive a double portion... and so they will inherit a double portion in their land..."

Isaiah 61:7, excerpts, NIV

"Enlarge the place of your tent, stretch your tent curtains wide, do not hold back; lengthen your cords, strengthen your stakes. For you will spread out to the right and to the left..."

Isaiah 54:2-3b, NIV

The Moses Connection

Moses and Ezekiel, both Levites, played a very unique historical role: declaring overall border assignments for Israel and determining how the tribal land allocations would be made. Compare these two events of the Lord's land-assignment instructions:

> *[God speaking:] "This will be your land, with its boundaries on every side." Moses commanded the Israelites: "Assign this land by lot as an inheritance. The LORD has ordered that it be given to the nine and a half tribes..." The LORD said to Moses, "These are the names of the men who are to assign the land for you as an inheritance: Eleazar the priest and Joshua son of Nun. And appoint one leader from each tribe to help assign the land."*
> *Numbers 34:12b-13, 16-18, NIV*

> *This is what the Sovereign LORD says: "These are the boundaries by which you [Ezekiel, a priest[94]] are to divide the land for an inheritance among the twelve tribes of Israel, with two portions for Joseph. You are to divide it equally among them..."*
> *Ezekiel 47:13-14a, NIV*

Moses (through Eleazar) and Ezekiel were both acting in a priestly role in these activities. Another thing in common for these men is that both were also prophets. Moses was perhaps the greatest of all the prophets[95], and Ezekiel was clearly a prominent one. By these two avenues – priest *and* prophet – were these two men authorized by God to make Israel's land assignments.

We've just walked the baseline boundaries Ezekiel gave us, and they line up with those given by Moses. But now we know that Ezekiel's border descriptions not only confirmed those of Moses: they were just as divinely endorsed, as two independent "witnesses." The circumstances are similar as well: entering the Promised Land.

The point of all these parallels was not lost on Ezekiel's original hearers. Since the times of David and Solomon, the lands of Israel had gone through a steady reduction. By Ezekiel's time, Moses' border definitions seemed a long-forgotten dream, with the territory amounting to only a small portion of the southern kingdom of Judah. Ezekiel lived in the day when even these last vestiges of the promised dominion were lost to the Babylonians. This is why the

---

[94] Ezekiel 1:3.

[95] Deuteronomy 34:10.

notion of future reinstitution of Moses' borders was so astounding for him and his hearers, for it was a reaffirmation of God's original promises to Israel.

> *Because I swore with uplifted hand to give it to your forefathers, this land will become your inheritance.* [96]
> *Ezekiel 47:14b, NIV*

We have surveyed the edges of this "inheritance" with Ezekiel. And though there are some questions and oddities, we can be confident of having a reasonable grasp of what those final border definitions refer to. We have also seen God's authorization by which both Ezekiel and Moses defined these lines.

From these facts, we can see that where the "baseline" borders of Moses were expanded in his and Joshua-Yeshua's day, we can anticipate that the baseline map of Ezekiel *will see analogous expansions in the day of Joshua-Yeshua to come.* Put simply, we need to back-track a bit and re-survey a certain section of our border. For reasons mentioned above, and more that we will discover, we've not quite defined the south-eastern line.

Reacquisitions, Part 1

Moses' descriptions for the original borders for the south-east section were, as all the rest, very similar to those declared by Ezekiel. After having come down between the Damascus and Hauran districts, and turning towards Galilee,

> *Then the boundary will go down along the Jordan and end at the Salt [Dead] Sea. This will be your land, with its boundaries on every side.*
> *Numbers 34:12, NIV*

You can read for yourself the remainder of those initially promised boundaries in Numbers 34, and see how similar Ezekiel's information is. You will also notice that what follows is a vital caveat:

> *The LORD said to Moses, 2 "Command the Israelites and say to them: 'When you enter Canaan,* ***the land that will be allotted to you as an inheritance will have these boundaries...*** *' " [border description follows.] 13 Moses commanded the Israelites: "Assign this land by lot as an inheritance. The LORD has ordered that it be given to the nine and a half tribes, 14* ***because the families of the tribe of Reuben, the tribe of Gad and the half-tribe***

[96] See Genesis 22:16-18 and Exodus 32:13.

of Manasseh have received their inheritance. *15* ***These two and a half tribes have received their inheritance on the east side of the Jordan of Jericho, toward the sunrise."***
Numbers 34:1-2, 13-15, NIV

What this says is that the borders first promised to Israel were inherently appended by regions on Jordan's *eastern* side, *territories already in their possession.* These areas did not need to be mentioned in the main enumerations because their inclusion went without saying: they were a *fait accompli.* Having just conquered the Amorite peoples governed by Og and Sihon[97], but even *before* the Jordan was crossed, Israel already occupied these lands; they were already part of her "inheritance." Though no mention is made in Moses' "map," they were every bit counted with Israel's inheritance as the rest.

In the land area of Israel to come, a similar phenomenon can be therefore expected. Ezekiel, speaking in a role similar to that of Moses, describes Israel's land after "the dust has settled" in a mighty battle for the Holy Land[98]. If any territories will have been already taken in this battle, they will apparently – just as in Moses' day, and for the same reasons – be added to the Ezekiel baseline.

Reacquisitions, Part 2

Since, during Joshua's time, the Amorite lands of Og and Sihon were added to Israel's "inheritance," will the same phenomenon take place during Yeshua's coming victory? In answer, we can consult another of our guides, a contemporary of Ezekiel's in fact. This man Daniel, also living in exile in Babylon, prophesied:

He [the false messiah] will also enter the Beautiful Land, and many countries will fall; but ***these will be rescued out of his hand: Edom, Moab and the foremost of the sons of Ammon.***
Daniel 11:41, NASB

The setting here is just before the King, Yeshua-Jesus, returns; the "he" referred to above will have been the greatest oppressor of God's people in all history: a "beast" of a man, commonly referred to as "Antichrist" by Christians[99]. Daniel is describing that profane ruler in the tumultuous time just prior to

---

[97] E.g., Joshua 12-13.

[98] Ezekiel 38-39.

[99] Per, e.g., 1 John 2:18, 4:3, in connection with passages such as 2 Thessalonians 2:3 and Revelation 13:1-10.

Messiah's ultimate deliverance of His people[100]. It is very interesting that, in a day when the most evil emperor in history gains sway over many nations and most rulers of the earth[101], there is specifically singled out three tiny and ancient countries that escape his destruction: Edom, Ammon and Moab. Though Daniel does not explain why these lands are singled out for "escape" from "the Beast," that he does so is enough of a red flag in itself.

But there are more ties to our story, and more red flags, beginning with the special origins of these nations and their almost literal relationships with Israel. For once upon a time, Israel (Jacob), Edom (Esau), Ammon and Moab were four individual men, closely related to Abraham, and therefore to one another. Esau (Edom) was Israel's brother; Ammon and Moab the sons of Isaac's first cousin, Lot. Eventually, nations were created through their offspring, and territories were assigned by God to each[102].

Though related nations, all three denied access to Israel in her original entry to the Promised Land. Worse, all three exulted when Israel (i.e., the last hope of Judah and Jerusalem) was destroyed by the Babylonians in 586 B.C.[103] and effectually ejected from the Promised Land. In between those events, all three "relatives" were a perpetual thorn in Israel's side.

But for some reason, in a time yet to come, we have seen that these three ancient territories will be exempted from Antichrist's control. Why? Could it be that they are being preserved for "special treatment" by God? Are they being singled out for Israel's occupation? Apparently so: for in this period, such dominance will have taken place:

> *And it shall come to pass in that day, that the root of Jesse, that standeth for an ensign of the peoples, unto him shall the nations seek; and his resting-place shall be glorious. 11 And it shall come to pass in that day, that the Lord will set his hand again the second time to recover the remnant of his people… 12 And he will set up an ensign for the nations, and will assemble the outcasts of Israel, and gather together the dispersed of Judah from the four corners of the earth. 14…* ***together shall they*** *[Israel]* ***despoil the children of the east: they shall put forth their hand upon Edom and Moab; and the children of Ammon shall obey them.***
> *Isaiah 11:10-11a,12,14b, ASV*

---

[100] Daniel 12:1-3.

[101] E.g., Daniel 11:40-42; Revelation 16:14.

[102] E.g., Deuteronomy 2:9, 19: "*I have given it as a possession to the descendants of Lot.*"

[103] Ammon: see Jeremiah 49:1; Ezekiel 21:28, 25:2-5; Amos 1:13. Moab: see Jeremiah 48:1-2; Ezekiel 25:8-11; cf Amos 2:1-2. Edom: see Lamentations 4:21; Ezekiel 25:12; Amos 1:11-12.

So let's put this all together. In the context of the apocalyptic battle to come, Messiah (the descendent "root" of Jesse and Son of David), will draw His people from all nations and gather them as His "remnant." In that very context, even before the smoke has cleared, and under Yeshua's command, those gathered from Israel (specifically "of Judah," Jews) will take over a large area just eastward of the Jordan. That area is comprised of the ancient territories of Edom, Moab and Ammon.

This land acquisition comes not during post-conflict assignments, but as a direct and immediate consequence of the battle. Just as with the initial entering into the Promised Land, Israel will have already possessed these east-of-Jordan holdings, even *before* the full resettling of the Holy Land takes place.

Exactly as in the time of Joshua of old, Yeshua-Joshua will complete the task. Exactly as Moses described Israel's borders, those described by Ezekiel are automatically added to lands already held, east of the Jordan. Such prior holdings lands were not contained in either prophet's description, for both apparently focused on the remainder that had yet to be assigned.

The next question is, of the ancient territories of Edom, Moab and Ammon, how much of it will future-Israel occupy? An initial answer might be that it would be the same real estate as it was at the first.

For background, and as illustrated below[104], the two-and-a-half eastern tribes took over the Amorite regions of Gilead and Bashan. Before and after, Moab and Ammon were to the east, with Edom to the south. Eventually, Moab and Ammon overpowered the two-and-a-half tribes' regions, and – for the bulk of First Testament history – occupied that land.

Armed with this, we can put the question better. Will future Israel occupy only her original tribal regions here? Or, will she embrace the entirety of ancient Edom, Moab and Ammon? In answer, a certain passage sheds a lot of light.

> *But ye, O mountains of Israel,* **ye shall shoot forth your branches**, *and yield your fruit to my people of Israel; for they are at hand to come. 9 For, behold, I am for you, and I will turn unto you, and ye shall be tilled and sown: 10 And I will multiply men upon you,* **all the house of Israel, even all of it**: *and* **the cities shall be inhabited, and the wastes shall be builded**: *11 And I will multiply upon you man and beast; and they shall increase and bring fruit:* **and I will settle you after your old estates, and will do better unto you than at your beginnings**: *and* **ye shall know that I am the LORD**.
> *Ezekiel 36:8-11, KJV*

---

104 Tribal borders based on Beitzel, Barry J. "Map 31: Tribal Distribution of Palestine." The Moody Atlas of Bible Lands, Chicago, IL, Moody Publishers, Inc, 2000. Tracing by me, with permission.

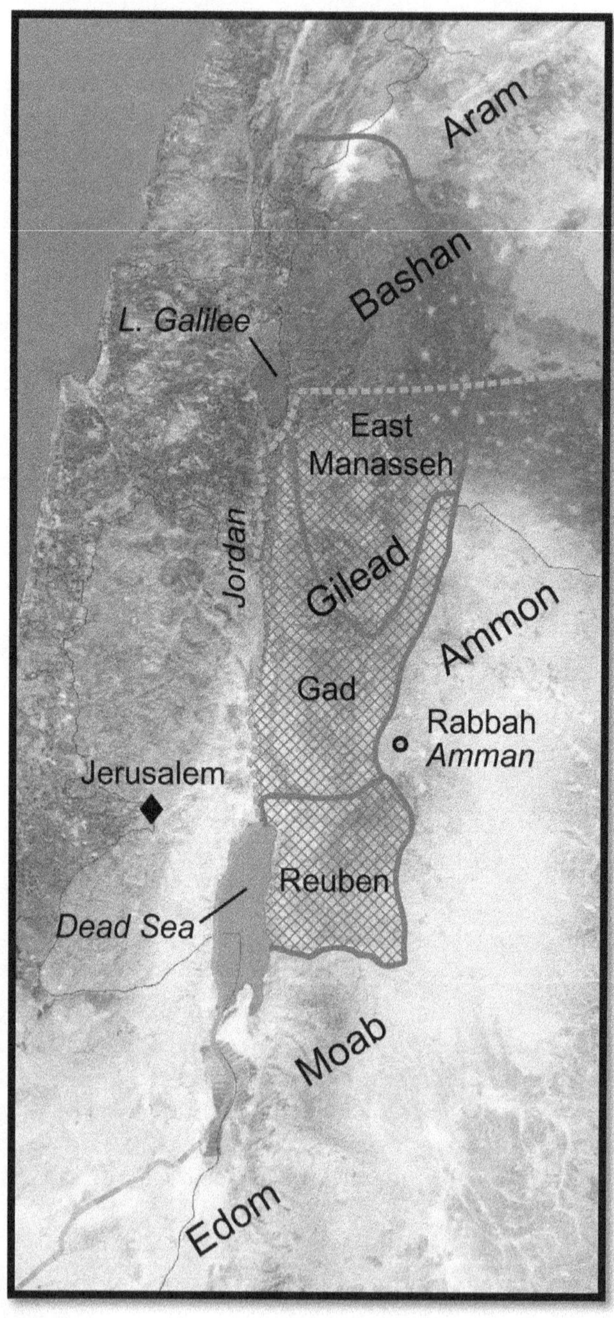

Figure 5: The Eastern Tribes

Our guide Ezekiel prophesies several key things in this very same setting of Israel's coming fulfillment. Firstly, the Lord will re-establish the habitations of original Israel in times to come, including "all the house": that is, including those "eastern" tribes of Reuben, Gad, and the half-tribe of Manasseh. Those lands east of the Jordan, Gilead and Bashan[105] must be included, for they were originally part of Israel's "old estates."

But let's keep another point in mind though. In regards these "estates," the Lord "*will do better unto you than at your beginnings.*" Because of the battle conquests of Edom, Moab and Ammon, when God does "*better unto* [Israel] *than at* [Israel's] *beginnings*," she may very well keep the entirety of these regions as part of her "portion."

Blessed Settlements

With the foregoing prophecies, one might get the idea that these border arrangements will be accomplished by some sort of raw military empowerment for contemporary Israel. However, when the prophecies unfold the results will speak not to human strength, but to our Lord's sovereignty over all the nations and all creation. Just as with the original Passover, Exodus and entry to the Promised Land, the story will be about God's intervention, rescue and enablement; the glory will be His. From this perspective, when we consider how God says He feels about all this, there are further clues to enlargements of Israel's future borders.

The Lord's Victory

In the original "sibling conflicts" between Jacob and Esau, and between Israel and his "second cousins" of Moab and Ammon, there was not only a conflict with Jacob-Israel[106], but with God Himself. Inhabitants of these regions were generally hostile to *His* purposes, from Israel's initial entry into the Promised Land to her exit from it during the Babylonian invasion. When these same areas are reacquired in the future, the Lord's pleasure is evident:

[105] Bashan and Gilead were nations with practices so despicable that God decided to remove them entirely and give their land to Israel (e.g., Amos 2:9-10).

[106] The initial nation that God created for himself: e.g., Deuteronomy 4:34.

God has spoken from his sanctuary: "In triumph I will parcel out Shechem and measure off the Valley of Succoth. ***Gilead*** *is mine, and* ***Manasseh*** *is mine; Ephraim is my helmet, Judah my scepter.* ***Moab*** *is my washbasin, upon* ***Edom*** *I toss my sandal; over Philistia I shout in triumph."*
Psalms 60:6-8 (and 108:7-9), NIV

"But I will bring Israel back to his own pasture and he will graze on Carmel and ***Bashan****; his appetite will be satisfied on the hills of Ephraim and* ***Gilead****. In those days, at that time," declares the LORD, "search will be made for Israel's guilt, but there will be none, and for the sins of Judah, but none will be found, for I will forgive the remnant I spare."*
Jeremiah 50:19-20, NIV

Both these passages are quotations of the Lord Himself; both are set in a future time of final outworking of His program, with perfection seen in the loving obedience of God's people[107]. From both passages, regions east of the Jordan will clearly be involved in Israel's jurisdiction in the Messianic era:

- Succoth was on the *east* side of the Jordan, north of the Dead Sea on the Jabbok River.
- Gilead is the land *east* of the Jordan, from Galilee southwards.
- Manasseh (for one half of that tribe) resided *east* of the Jordan.
- Bashan refers to that land *east* of Galilee and the Jordan, extending north above Gilead.

The simple message is that when all is said and done, the Lord will prevail over all who have resisted Him. In Biblical times, there were plenty of trans-Jordan conflicts. But when related matters are settled in history ahead, there will be a finality about it that satisfies Adonai Himself. For all the insults hurled against Creator-God, over time, by various groups east of the Jordan, He will satisfy *Himself.*

For this reason, we see once again that a significant section of what is now south-western Jordan will be integrated into the territory of Israel, in Messiah's day. The Lord will Himself re-establish Israel upon her original lands, which include that of the two-and-a-half tribes originally settled east of the Jordan, and much of the area occupied by Edom, Moab and Ammon.

107 Cf Jeremiah 31, etc.

Neighbors Restored

Does this Lord's victory mean that all memory of these three nations will be eradicated? Well, practically speaking, it already is. For how often does Edom, Moab or Ammon show up in the evening news? The more interesting question is, will the Lord actually resurrect these nations in the day of His reign? In some passages there might be hints to the affirmative[108], while in others perhaps an emphatic negative[109]. So there is more than meets the eye to this topic, and we have to dig a little deeper. Consider the following:

> *"Therefore, as I live," declares the Lord of hosts, the God of Israel, "Surely Moab will be like Sodom, and the sons of Ammon like Gomorrah — A place possessed by nettles and salt pits, and a perpetual desolation. The remnant of My people will plunder them, and the remainder of My nation will inherit them."*
> *Zephaniah 2:9, NASB*

> *"And Edom will become an object of horror; everyone who passes by it will be horrified and will hiss at all its wounds. 18 Like the overthrow of Sodom and Gomorrah with its neighbors," says the Lord, "no one will live there, nor will a son of man reside in it."*
> *Jeremiah 49:17-18, NASB*

Being prophetically compared to Sodom and Gomorrah, in regards to punishment, is not a good thing for any country: it pretty much means that area is geologically obliterated, and the people associated with it are gone for good. Even so, in the context of Messiah's Day, after a long period of punishment,

> *"Yet I will restore the fortunes of Moab in the latter days," declares the Lord.*
> *Jeremiah 48:47a, NASB*

> *"But afterward I will restore the fortunes of the sons of Ammon," Declares the Lord.*
> *Jeremiah 49:6, NASB*

Are there similar prophecies for Edom? Not so much. But for the other two, let's not miss the point that God may well "resurrect" a remnant of Moab and Ammon, as distinct peoples. Just from the genetic standpoint, that is a rather

---

[108] E.g., Daniel 11:41.
[109] E.g., Ezekiel 25:8-14; Malachi 1:4.

astounding prophecy. But regardless of who those people will be, their land will apparently be that of south-eastern Jordan.

If God can "restore the fortunes" of dead nations such as Moab and Ammon, He can surely heal and strengthen any nation that calls upon Him. We see this for Millennial Israel's ancient southern and northern neighbors, Egypt and Assyria. Isaiah gives us a truly startling glimpse of how important Egypt and Assyria will be in the Millennial era, and how enthusiastic their participation:

> *In that day there will be a highway from Egypt to Assyria, and the Assyrians will come into Egypt and the Egyptians into Assyria, and the Egyptians will worship [the Lord*[110]*] with the Assyrians. 24* ***In that day Israel will be the third party with Egypt and Assyria, a blessing in the midst of the earth,*** *25 whom the Lord of hosts has blessed, saying, "****Blessed is Egypt My people, and Assyria the work of My hands, and Israel My inheritance.****"*
> *Isaiah 19:23-25, NASB*

Clearly, Israel is not the only country that God is, or will be, proud of. Egypt and Assyria will eagerly involve themselves, in ongoing fashion, with worship of the Lord. In fact, the Bible seems to point out Egypt as an example of how all the nations will worship Him in their own lands[111].

Given the key roles that these three countries will play, it is understandable that clear borders are emphasized between them. The "river" of Egypt (Wadi el-Arish, not the Nile) and *the* River (the Euphrates) are consistently upheld as *final* and ultimate borders for Israel (even after all expansions), with these two "blessed" countries beyond those watercourses.

Prospering in the Lord's Glory

However the borders of Israel (and all other nations) are finally laid out, we can know that it is the Prince of Peace who will call the shots: very firmly[112], but with complete fairness and full appreciation of the people and circumstances concerned[113]. The wisdom and equity that Yeshua will display will have had no precedence in history – except for glimpses perhaps in the foreshadowing work of His "brother," Solomon[114].

[110] See context.
[111] Read Isaiah 19:18-22, with Zechariah 14:16-19 and Zephaniah 2:11.
[112] E.g., "with an iron scepter": Psalms 2:9; Revelation 12:5, 19:15.
[113] E.g., Isaiah 2:4; Micah 4:3.
[114] Compare Luke 11:31 with (e.g.) 1 Kings 10:23 / 2 Chronicles 9:22.

People of every nation and language will bow to the coming King and confess that He is Lord[115]. Those that do so willingly, as with Egypt and Assyria[116], will find themselves wonderfully blessed. And who knows? There is "room" in the prophecies for even Ammon and Moab seek the Lord, and find His salvation and blessing.

> ***And everyone who calls on the name of the Lord will be saved;*** *for on Mount Zion and in Jerusalem there will be deliverance, as the Lord has said, among* ***the survivors whom the Lord calls.***
> *Joel 2:32, NIV*[117]

No matter what, and after all is settled in the brief Apocalyptic transition, the nations of Ammon, Moab, and every other will find their lands defined and restored to them by the King of all kings. The Prince of Peace will rule all nations with equity, with satisfaction all around. All of this will redound not to human cleverness or mightiness, but to the strong wisdom and powerful love embodied in the God-King soon to come:

> *Thy [Israel's / Jacob's] people also shall be all righteous; they shall inherit the land for ever, the branch of my planting, the work of* ***my*** *hands,* ***that I may be glorified.***
> *Isaiah 60:21, ASV*

In the end, Israel's borders will declare the *Lord's* Word that is active across all history. Though the Promised Land will once more embrace lands lying to the east of the Jordan River, the ultimate purpose will not be a declaration of Israel's preeminence, or an assistance of her economy. Rather, the expansion will speak first and foremost to the Lord's own glory and faithfulness, in that the work of *His* hands will have been fully, finally and lastingly accomplished.

---

115 Isaiah 45:23; Romans 14:11; Philippians 2:10-11.

116 Presumably composed of what are now portions of Syria and the bulk of Iraq.

117 Also Acts 2:21; Romans 10:13

The Father's Conquests

David Returning

Beyond the law of the firstborn, a different legal matter applies to our expedition, and it involves a *royal* birthright from a particular ancient ancestor. Our main guide, Ezekiel, emphasizes that king of old, saying he would once more rule – in the very period ahead that we are interested in.

> *I will place over them one shepherd, my servant* ***David****, and he will tend them; he will tend them and be their shepherd. I the LORD will be their God, and my servant* ***David*** *will be* ***prince***[118] *among them. I the LORD have spoken.*
> *Ezekiel 34:23-24, NIV*

> *My servant* ***David*** *will be* ***king*** *over them, and they will all have one shepherd. They will follow my laws and be careful to keep my decrees. They will live in the land I gave to my servant Jacob, the land where your fathers lived. They and their children and their children's children will live there forever, and* ***David*** *my servant will be their* ***prince*** *forever.*
> *Ezekiel 37:24-25, NIV*

The Son Fulfilling the Role of the Father

In ancient Biblical parlance (and perhaps other cultures to this day), being the son of a man involves extending the blood and life[119] of that man into the future, enabling, in a sense, the father's days to be extended. This is particularly true with royal bloodlines, where the authority and other regal attributes of the forebears are transmitted to successive generations.

With this in mind, let's consider the coming Prince: *Yeshua ha Mashiach*, *Joshua* the *Messiah*, *Iesous Christos*, *Jesus* the *Christ*, *Jesus the son of David.* Though not

---

[118] Several English Bibles use the term "Prince" in the passages of Ezekiel (40-48) we will be working with. However, the Hebrew term *nasi'* (Strong's OT:5387) stems from the idea of "exalted one," and can be rendered as "king," ruler," "prince," "sheik," "captain," etc. Even so, the rendition "Prince" will be retained here, for it underscores Messiah's being the prophesied Son of (king) David and heir to his throne.

[119] "The life is in the blood." See Leviticus 17:10, Deuteronomy 12:23.

generally recognized as such in His day[120], Jesus was (through Mary) a literal descendant of David. Regardless, He received all the royal authority, titles and claims of King David; and since He is not dead[121], and had no heirs[122], Jesus retains to this day all rights to David's throne. Thus it is that Ezekiel could say David is "returning": for through his living descendent, he is.

David was both a warrior and poet; both a lofty king, and a man whose humble heart was entirely bound up with the Lord's[123]. God therefore upheld his royal lineage throughout the history of the kingdom of Judah. "David," through his "Son," has already come as *mashiach* (messiah, anointed) priest. It remains, however, for Jesus (Joshua, *Yeshua*, meaning "Yahweh is Deliverance") to return in the ultimate role of His father David: as anointed king. It is this coming of the *mashiach* Prince to which so many prophecies look:

> *"The days are coming," declares the LORD, "when I will raise up to David a righteous Branch, a King who will reign wisely and do what is just and right in the land. In his days Judah will be saved and Israel will live in safety. This is the name by which he will be called: The LORD Our Righteousness."*
> *Jeremiah 23:5-6, NIV*

> *In those days and at that time I will make a righteous Branch sprout from David's line; he will do what is just and right in the land. In those days Judah will be saved and Jerusalem will live in safety. This is the name by which it will be called: The LORD Our Righteousness.*
> *Jeremiah 33:15-16, NIV*

> *Afterward the Israelites will return and seek the LORD their God and David their king. They will come trembling to the LORD and to his blessings in the last days.*
> *Hosea 3:5, NIV*

> *In that day I will restore David's fallen tent. I will repair its broken places, restore its ruins, and build it as it used to be…*
> *Amos 9:11, NIV*

---

[120] Many of the common folk, however, did recognize Jesus as the Son of David, with all that title's ramifications. E.g., Matthew 9:27, 12:23, 15:22, 20:30-31, 21:9, 21:15, 22:41.
[121] The entire point of the New Testament is Jesus' resurrection, after having paid the price for our sins as the Lamb of God.
[122] E.g., Isaiah 53:8.
[123] 1 Samuel 13:14; 1 Kings 11:4; Acts 13:22.

The Prince to come, the Son of David, came to Earth and became the salvation for all mankind as our sacrifice[124]. Indeed, when He comes again, he will be recognized as the one who had been pierced[125]. But next time, Jesus will come in royal power. He will reign over this world with the strength and spirit of His natural father[126] and with all the power of God.

> *For to us a child is born, to us a son is given, and the government will be on his shoulders. And* **he will be called** *Wonderful Counselor,* **Mighty God,** *Everlasting Father,* **Prince of Peace.** *Of the increase of his government and peace there will be no end.* **He will reign on David's throne and over his kingdom, establishing and upholdin***g it with justice and righteousness from that time on and forever. The zeal of the LORD Almighty will accomplish this.*
> *Isaiah 9:6-7, NIV*

Mapping Implications

While there are many spiritual lessons in all of this, we must return to the practical mapping implications. Coming in the role of conquering and anointed (*mashiach*) king, The Prince will be fully authorized in all things related to David's rule, and "*will reign on David's throne and over his kingdom.*" In regards to Israel's coming territory, we should therefore expect that the lands that King David dominated will also be held by Messiah, for He *will rule over nothing less than what his natural ancestor David attained.*

For these reasons, the extended boundaries of Israel under David (the Prince's natural "father") and Solomon (the Prince's foreshadowing "brother") are now on the table. These borders extended far beyond those originally declared through Ezekiel (and Moses before him) for Israel's "inheritance." As illustrated in the following map[127], three distinct regions are now worth considering.

---

124 See Isaiah 53 for a graphic description of His prophesied suffering, in the achievement of such a salvation for us.

125 Psalms 22:16; Isaiah 53:5; Zechariah 12:10; John 19:37.

126 That is, via His being born of Mary, a descendant of David.

127 David's and Solomon's borders based on Beitzel, Barry J. "Map 46: The Kingdom of David and Solomon," The Moody Atlas of Bible Lands, Chicago, IL, Moody Publishers, Inc, 2000. Tracing by me, with permission.

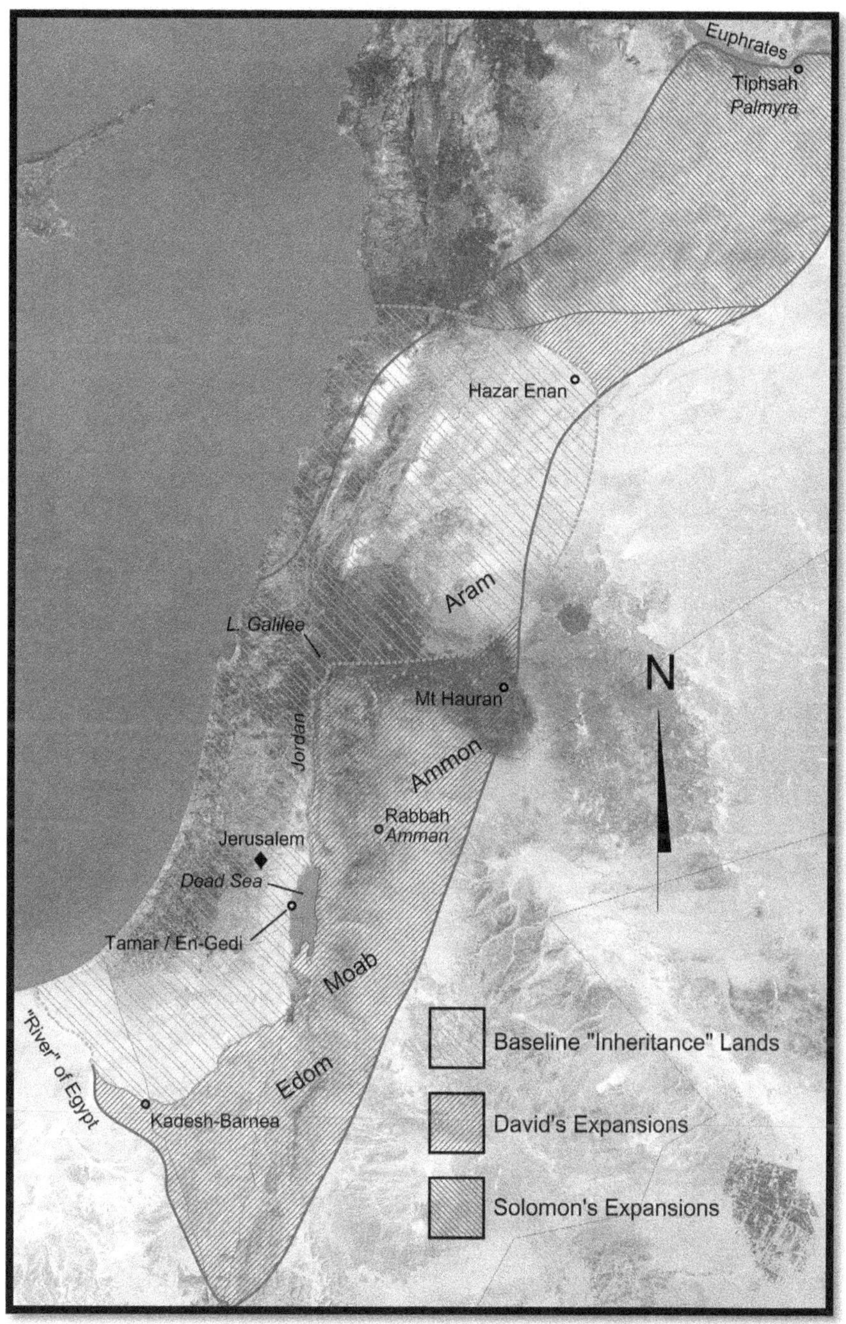

Figure 6: Monarchical Expansions

As can be seen, these three areas are:

- The "baseline" map already surveyed.
- Regions nationally expanded by, or brought under submission to, King David. Note that the east-of-Jordan reacquisitions are easily contained by this area.
- Regions brought under submission to David's son Solomon.

The south-eastern "Davidic" area equates with scriptures we have already seen that speak of Israel's taking of the lands of Moab, Ammon and at least northern Edom.

In the southern extension toward the Red Sea, we see an interesting conformance with *modern* borders. We also see a complete takeover of ancient Edom, in conformance with the prophecies of victory over that particular ancient enemy.

Also interesting is the squaring off of the north-west corner. This, with the southern dominion[128] of David, certainly brings a more regular shape to the land, with Jerusalem and the Jordan more central.

Lands of the "Brother"

The northernmost area indicated is that which David, by way of his "direct" heir Solomon, further expanded his dominion.

> *And Solomon ruled over all the kingdoms from the [Euphrates[129]] River to the land of the Philistines, as far as the border of Egypt. These countries brought tribute and were Solomon's subjects all his life… For he ruled over all the kingdoms west of the [Euphrates] River, from Tiphsah to Gaza, and had peace on all sides.*
> *1 Kings 4:21, 24, NIV*

> *He ruled over all the kings from the [Euphrates] River to the land of the Philistines, as far as the border of Egypt.*
> *2 Chronicles 9:26, NIV*

---

128 Israel did not *occupy* all of the south-east region indicated. Instead, Moab, Ammon and Edom were subject to David, their lands therefore being considered as under his domination.

129 Being the huge river of rivers from the perspective of Middle East, the Euphrates is often referred to in the Bible as simply "the River," with the various contexts demonstrating that it is the Euphrates in view.

This lengthy northern thrust was not unexpected. God, in an additional word through Moses, declared that the originally-established baseline would indeed be appended in exactly this fashion:

> ***I will establish your borders from the Red Sea to the Sea of the Philistines, and from the desert to the*** *[Euphrates]* ***River.*** *I will hand over to you the people who live in the land and you will drive them out before you.*
> *Exodus 23:31, NIV*

Yes, Solomon fulfilled this prophecy. But his conquests were but a foreshadowing of his "brother" to come. For as Solomon himself prophesied, the coming Messiah would accomplish something even greater. His rule will be not from the Euphrates to the (southern) desert, but from that river to the ends of the earth:

> *In his days the righteous will flourish; prosperity will abound till the moon is no more.* ***He will rule from sea to sea and from the*** *[Euphrates]* ***River to the ends of the earth.***
> *Psalms 72:7-8, NIV*

In another confirmation, the prophet Zechariah tells us:

> *I will take away the chariots from Ephraim and the war-horses from Jerusalem, and the battle bow will be broken. He will proclaim peace to the nations.* ***His rule will extend from sea to sea and from the*** *[Euphrates]* ***River to the ends of the earth.***
> *Zechariah 9:10, NIV*

As foreshadowed by the achievements of Solomon, and in final fulfillment to these prophecies, we can anticipate that Messiah's dominion will be expanded northward to touch at least some portion of the Euphrates River.

The Idea of Doubling

As a final consideration for expansions of the Holy Land under Messiah, there is that of the "doubled portion" belonging to the "firstborn." This is a divinely-inaugurated legal matter, and will most likely apply to the nation of Israel as a whole and specifically to the real estate she will ultimately occupy.

Since this topic is a bit of a side excursion, it is dealt with in Appendix A: Firstborn's Portion." If you feel the need for background details, please read that section now. Otherwise, the summary is that Israel occupies a "firstborn" position amongst all the nations, and is thus referred to by God as His "firstborn son." As such, the law of the firstborn comes into play, requiring an eventual double portion of land, specifically, a doubling of the area described by Moses and confirmed by Ezekiel.

How does this legal "doubling" of real estate compare with what we just saw for the "Davidic" expansions? Quite well, for a doubling of Ezekiel's prophesied geography is indeed on a par with the area dominated by David-Solomon, in the height of Solomon's rule.

It is in this light that a passage describing the coming Son of David gains additional meaning:

> ***I will also appoint him*** *[David's descendent]* ***my firstborn, the most exalted of the kings of the earth.*** *I will maintain my love to him forever, and my covenant with him will never fail.*
> *Psalms 89:27, NIV*

With the fulfillment of the law of the firstborn in Messiah's time, and in regards to doubling of territory, there is therefore a fulfillment of legal rights to two kinds of "firstborn": Israel, the Lord's nation-"son," and the Prince who is also the *actual* Son of God. David's son, Yeshua, will have been "appointed" the "firstborn" of the Father-God. As God's own firstborn[130], Jesus will therefore obtain His own doubled portion as King, a doubling of land-inheritance similar in scope to what David (and Solomon) accomplished.

At the same time, His people, Jacob-Israel, will finally receive "his" double portion as well:

> *Instead of their shame my people will receive a* **double portion**, *and instead of disgrace they will rejoice in their inheritance; and so* **they will inherit a double portion in their land**, *and everlasting joy will be theirs.*
> *Isaiah 61:7, NIV*

> *As for you, because of the blood of my covenant with you, I will free your prisoners from the waterless pit. Return to your fortress, O prisoners of hope;* ***even now I announce that I will restore twice as much to you.***
> *Zechariah 9:11-12, NIV*

[130] CF 1 Corinthians 15:20,22.

Adjusting the Map

Geographic Impact

Will the geographical area of Millennial Israel be exactly twice as much as that described by Moses and Ezekiel? We cannot know for sure. But when our Prince reigns, we can know that He will expand His direct dominion[131] to at least that obtained by His "father" David and His "brother" Solomon.

Now, there is a difference between the actual borders of Israel and the broader area of direct rule. For example, David did not eradicate Moab and Ammon, but held them (and therefore their lands) as subject to him. We cannot rule out the same sort of thing happening under David's "son." So the question is, for our purposes, how much of David's dominion will actually be annexed by, and inhabited by, future Israel? Though we cannot be positive at this time, there are some factors that have bearing.

- **Repeated tribal limitations.** As we will see in the next chapter, and in describing Dan's and Gad's boundaries, the northern and southern borders for all Israel are simultaneously reiterated, perhaps suggesting that these are quite firm.

- **The "River prophecies."** The many statements regarding the expansion north to the Euphrates, though sure, may refer to jurisdiction over vassal regions (vs. an annexation), as with Solomon's rule.

- **East-West Non-Conformity.** All the tribal provinces will have (as we will see) a strict east-west design. The "Solomonic" Euphrates extension does not connect westward to the Mediterranean, and (if annexed to Israel) would seriously violate this apparent design intent. A similar point can be made for the extension south to the Red Sea.

[131] As distinct from His being King of all the world's kings, and that additional layer of global dominion, we are still referring to the country of Israel which Messiah will rule as *national* king.

- **Mega-Dan unlikely.** If the Euphrates extension were annexed, the northern-most tribe's (Dan's) west-most starting point would apparently remain just north of Tripoli, with tribal provinces to the south maintaining their east-west layout. This would require that Dan that bumps way north to the Euphrates, creating a mega-province that far overshadows the others and contradicting the command for equality in their assignments[132].

- **Mega-Gad unlikely.** For similar reasons, but to a lesser degree, a full annexation of Edom (south to the Red Sea) would presumably be taken in by the southernmost tribe: Gad. Again, such a singling out for enlargement seems highly unlikely. The alternative, dividing the extra land equally between the southern tribes, would seem to violate the strictly east-west patterns of boundaries between them.

- **Eastward expansion is not as limited.** Unlike the north and south borders, and the western coastline, the eastern border is not as fixed. For example, we are practically commanded to add the re-acquired tribal lands east of Jordan, pushing Ezekiel's border eastward from the Jordan. With the many prophecies of Edom, Moab and Ammon being obtained by Israel, there is even more probability of actual annexation in that south-eastern sector.

The details of the outworking are, of course, up to the Prince. Even so, God's Word has given us an amazing body of facts to consider.

A Working Theory

Since this is also a graphic expedition of sorts, we still need to come up with a working map that at least tries to account for the findings above. Again, the final borders are up to the Lord. But in summary, here are some final opinions on map adjustments.

The northern extension to the Euphrates will be considered here as a special vassal territory under Messiah's direct rule, just as it was for Solomon. The main reason for *not* annexing these lands is to avoid making an odd mega-province out of Dan. Not part of Israel proper and not fully inhabited by her citizens, for reasons known to God this region will be important for the Prince's purposes, in fulfillment of so many prophecies.

---

132 Ezekiel 47:13.

David's eastward dominion of Ammon, Moab and northern Edom *will* be considered here as fully annexed by Israel, per the many prophecies regarding Israel's takeover of those ancient territories. By way of precedence and prophecy, the odd "P"-shape of Ezekiel's border is filled in. This results in better equality in real estate for the various tribal provinces, granting the southern tribes a similar eastward expansion as the northern. Further, the arrangement allows Jerusalem and the Jordan to occupy a far more central position.

With this pattern of filling out to the east, and because it was also part of David's dominion, the northeast corner will also be considered as annexed.

As for David's southern extension to the Red Sea (by way of conquering Edom[133]), Gad will not be illustrated here as hugely extended in that direction, for reasons already discussed. Instead, like those provinces north of it, it will be extended eastward from the Jordan (and Dead Sea). Like the enlargement to the north, that reaching south to the Red Sea will be considered here as under special vassal status.

Again, the details will be up to the Prince. As a working model though, the following map illustrates arguments stated above. Referring to the next page, notice that the "vassal" regions touch the Euphrates and the Gulf of Aqaba. As a result, future Israel has access to three major bodies of water: the Mediterranean, the Red Sea and (via the Euphrates) the Persian Gulf. Notice also that the Euphrates was one of the four rivers flowing from original Eden, and that it's being touched by Messiah's garden-like (as we will see) realm to come may contain a big lesson or two.

For now though, we must press onward with the expedition. We have surveyed the overall borders, and seen how they will most likely be expanded. Now we will look at internal borders of the Holy Land to come.

---

[133] Evidenced in 2 Samuel 8:3-11 and 1 Chronicles 18:3-10. See Beitzel, Chapter 2, section entitled "King David's Exploits."

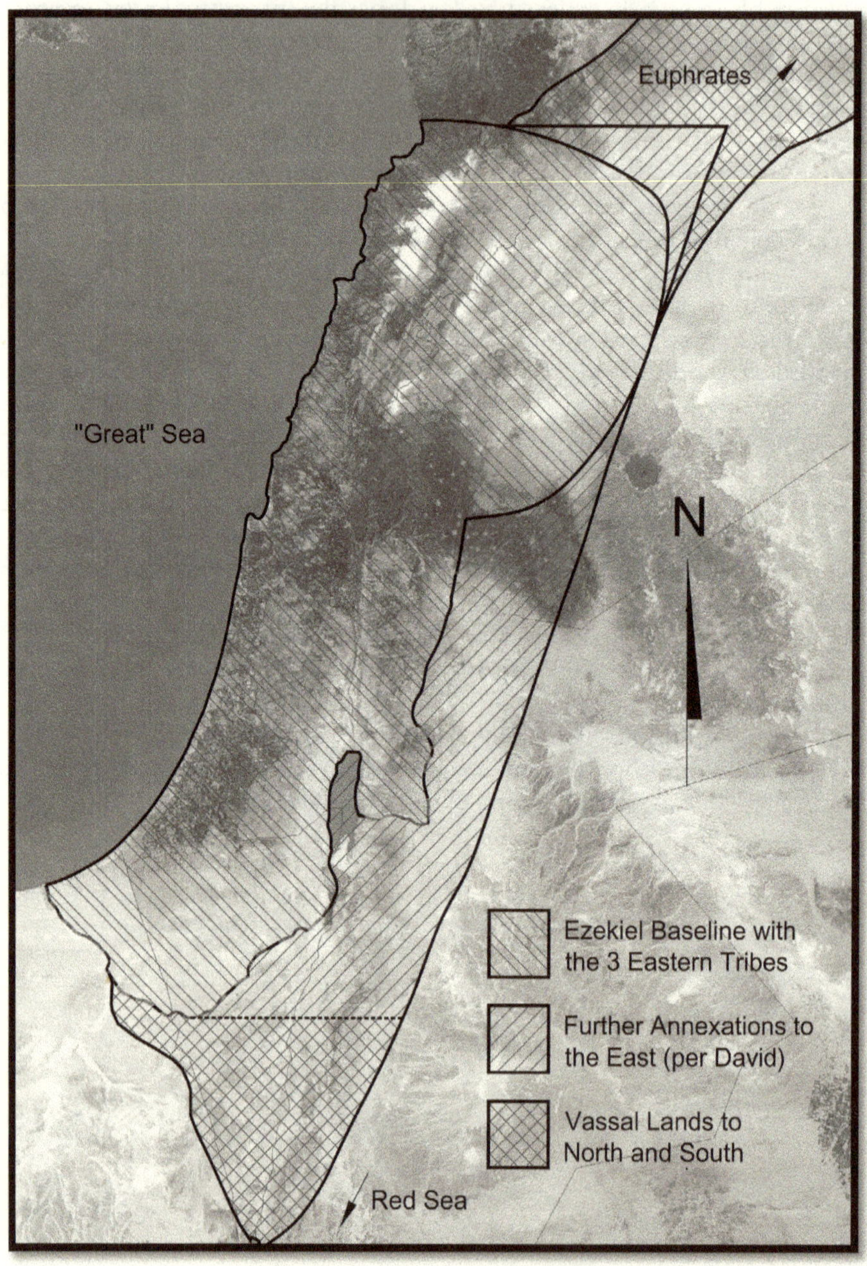

Figure 7: Expansion Summary

Chapter 4: Provincial Assignments

"This is the land you are to allot as an inheritance to the tribes of Israel, and these will be their portions," declares the Sovereign Lord.

Ezekiel 48:29, NIV

"You are to allot it as an inheritance for yourselves and for the aliens who have settled among you... In whatever tribe the alien settles, there you are to give him his inheritance," declares the Sovereign LORD.

Ezekiel 47:22a,23, NIV

Bulging at the Seams

Now on the verge of stepping in and going "cross-country," we are soon to witness how Millennial Israel is divided up and internally organized. We have geographic details, again offered by Ezekiel; but they are not quite complete. So to help fill in the blanks, we will first consider another key factor: internal population distribution, and how certain provinces might be affected in their relative size.

Why So Much Land?

In comparison with borders of contemporary Israel, the borders during Messiah's rule might seem quite large, perhaps four times the area. Some might think this excessive. However, it doesn't take much work to discover that the opposite may well be the case, in that the final borders may well be bulging at the seams with all the people there! For under the Millennial circumstances, even these future borders can be understood as fully populated, if not outgrown. To see why, let's begin with the Lord's gathering of all the Jewish faithful from *all* the world.

> ***In that day the Root of Jesse*** *[Messiah]* ***will stand as a banner for the peoples; the nations will rally to him, and his place of rest will be glorious.*** *11 In that day the Lord will reach out his hand a second time to reclaim the remnant that is left of his people from Assyria, from Lower Egypt, from Upper Egypt, from Cush, from Elam, from Babylonia, from Hamath and from the islands [distant coastlands] of the sea. 12* ***He will raise a banner for the nations and gather the exiles of Israel; he will assemble the scattered people of Judah from the four quarters of the earth.***
> *Isaiah 11:10-12, NIV*

Though the re-establishment and re-population of the country of Israel in recent times is an amazing and miraculous thing in itself, this "second" gathering, in the time of triumph of David's Son, will be even more impressive. The prophecy applies to any nation that Jews have been "scattered" to: "the four quarters of the earth." The Jewish population in Israel during Messiah's reign may therefore greatly outnumber those there today.

The Even Bigger Reason

There may be a much larger reason for population growth, because the ethnic Jewish population of Israel will be hugely augmented by others:

> ***You are to allot it as an inheritance for yourselves and for the aliens who have settled among you and who have children. You are to consider them as native-born Israelites;*** *along with you they are to be allotted an inheritance among the tribes of Israel. 23* ***In whatever tribe the alien settles, there you are to give him his inheritance,"*** *declares the Sovereign LORD.*
> *Ezekiel 47:22-23, NIV*

In Messiah's day, any non-Jewish believer can apparently immigrate to Israel and expect an opportunity of land "inheritance" there. Now, *that* will result in a big population jump, and a corresponding need for additional properties. This strict command through Ezekiel is not without precedent: for it was what God commanded through Moses when Israel first entered the Promised Land:

> ***The alien living with you must be treated as one of your native-born.*** *Love him as yourself, for you were aliens in Egypt. I am the LORD your God.*
> *Leviticus 19:34, NIV*

> *And you are to love those who are aliens, for you yourselves were aliens in Egypt.*
> *Deuteronomy 10:19, NIV*

With the coming and final land of promise, Ezekiel makes it clear that the requirement is being reestablished.

Why would Israel want foreign citizens in her midst, let alone love them? The answer, from the above verses, is that the "alien" (non-Israelite) neighbor serves as a living reminder of what the native-born were extracted from, by the hand of the Lord[134]. Israel's attitude toward these "foreign" brothers and sisters will not therefore be arrogant, but appreciative:

[134] See also Exodus 22:21 and 23:9.

> *"Then you will say in your heart, 'Who bore me these? I was bereaved and barren; I was exiled and rejected. Who brought these up? I was left all alone, but these — where have they come from?'" This is what the Sovereign LORD says: "See, I will beckon to the Gentiles, I will lift up my banner to the peoples; they will bring your sons in their arms and carry your daughters on their shoulders.*
> *Isaiah 49:21-22, NIV*

This will not be a free-for-all, though: for foreign settlers in Israel must obey the same law as the native-born[135]; whatever province they settle in, they will apparently become a full member of that tribe[136]. It will be just like they are full-fledged citizens, because they are: by the blood of the Prince, who was the sacrificial Lamb for us all. These foreign residents of future Israel will stand as a reminder to the entire world that it is Yeshua, the Anointed, who makes this peace possible:

> *Therefore, remember that formerly you who are Gentiles by birth and called "uncircumcised" by those who call themselves "the circumcision" (that done in the body by the hands of men) — 12* ***remember that at that time you were separate from Christ, excluded from citizenship in Israel and foreigners*** *to the covenants of the promise, without hope and without God in the world. 13 But* ***now in Christ Jesus you who once were far away have been brought near through the blood of Christ.***
>
> *14* ***For he himself is our peace, who has made the two one and has destroyed the barrier, the dividing wall of hostility****, 15 by abolishing in his flesh the law with its commandments and regulations.* ***His purpose was to create in himself one new man out of the two, thus making peace****, 16 and in this one body to reconcile both of them to God through the cross, by which he put to death their hostility. 17* ***He came and preached peace to you who were far away and peace to those who were near.*** *18 For through him we both have access to the Father by one Spirit.*
>
> *19 Consequently,* ***you are no longer foreigners and aliens, but fellow citizens with God's people*** *and members of God's household, 20 built on the foundation of the apostles and prophets, with Christ Jesus himself as the chief cornerstone.*
> *Ephesians 2:11-20, NIV*

The multi-national living arrangements will demonstrate this peace and unity that only the Lord will have been able to achieve. Obviously, not everyone

---

[135] E.g., Exodus 12:48-49; Leviticus 24:22; Numbers 9:14, 15:15-16.
[136] Ezekiel 47:23.

will choose this "inheritance" option, deciding to simply dwell in the lands of God's assignment. But a lot of folks will.

So we have two big reasons to anticipate a population boom for Israel then: the final gathering of the Jewish faithful, and a massive influx of gentiles deciding to live with them, *as citizens of that country.* Suffice it to say that the borders declared through Ezekiel, even with expansions per David, will soon be bulging at the seams. This is why:

> *The children born during your [Zion, Jerusalem] bereavement will yet say in your hearing,* ***'This place is too small for us; give us more space to live in.'***
> *Isaiah 49:20, NIV*

> *I will bring them back from Egypt and gather them from Assyria. I will bring them to Gilead and Lebanon, and* ***there will not be room enough for them.***
> *Zechariah 10:10, NIV*

By several means though, we have seen how this population problem will be remedied by the Lord. By His decree and instruction, He will tell Israel:

> *"Enlarge the place of your tent, stretch your tent curtains wide, do not hold back; lengthen your cords, strengthen your stakes.* ***For you will spread out to the right and to the left...****"*
> *Isaiah 54:2-3b, NIV*

And so the nation shall.

Judah's Increase

One tribe in particular will see a huge membership in comparison to the others. There are two reasons for this: Jew and Gentile. We have already seen the Jewish reason Judah's relative size: *he will assemble the scattered people of Judah from the four quarters of the earth* (Isaiah 11:12b, NIV). The term "Jew" means "people of Judah", and there is a good reason why both have become a metaphor for the entirety of Israel: after the Assyrian sack of the Northern Kingdom, and after the subsequent Babylonian captivity of Judah, that was the tribe most represented.

That is why Israelites are, after two and a half millennia, referred to as "people of Judah." So while all tribes of Israel survive, Judah remains quite prominent. This explains the otherwise odd phrasing in the verse just cited, and reinforces the straightforward fact that the coming province of Judah will need to be *big.*

The other reason for Judah's larger size has also been touched on: foreign-born citizenry. Where will the "non-Jewish Israelites" of tomorrow settle? Per Ezekiel[137], in whatever tribal province they wish. But there may be one tribal area that will be the particular favorite: next to, or within, the province of Judah. Why? Because the only means by which we Gentiles who were "*excluded from the commonwealth* [legal citizenry] *of Israel*" would be "brought near" and made one with Israel is "*by the blood of Christ.*" In regards to literal bloodlines, Yeshua was (and remains) a descendent of Judah; and it is His blood we profess to take into ourselves during Eucharist-Communion[138], in the greatest blood-covenant that ever will have been made. Therefore, if a gentile believer argued to be a member of any of the tribes of Israel, it would be that of Judah.

A lesser reason for Judah's growth is basic popularity. Judah is the lion, the ruler:

> *The scepter will not depart from Judah, nor the ruler's staff from between his feet, until he comes to whom it belongs and the obedience of the nations is his.*
> *Genesis 49:10, NIV*

When "*he comes to whom it belongs,*" when Yeshua-Joshua-Jesus takes the scepter, many will find a huge affinity for the Judah province. They will have varied reasons, and good. And they will also need a place to settle down and make their homes. Of all the tribal provinces, this one will need some extra real estate to accommodate them all.

Provincial Order

As with any country, tomorrow's Holy Land will be stratified into sub-regions, analogous to our states or provinces of today. But as with ancient Israel, these sub-regions are defined for, and associated with, the tribes descended from Jacob's sons.

---

137 Ezekiel 47:22-23.

138 E.g., Matthew 26:27-29; Mark 14:23-25.

Overview of the Arrangement

After describing the overall borders of the land, Ezekiel addresses these tribal sub-regions. Moving north to south, here is a schematic diagram of their positions[139]:

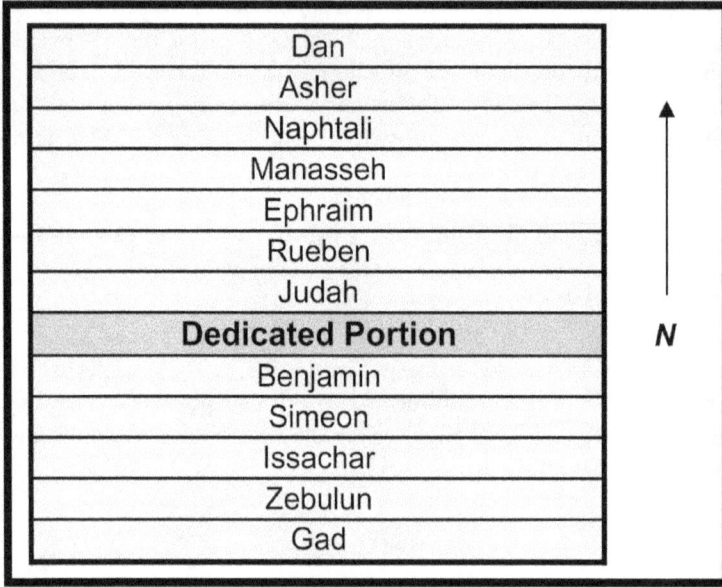

Dan
Asher
Naphtali
Manasseh
Ephraim
Rueben
Judah
Dedicated Portion
Benjamin
Simeon
Issachar
Zebulun
Gad

N

Figure 8: Divisions of the Provinces

In great contrast with the irregular shapes of Israel's ancient tribal borders, these "provinces" will be laid out in strict east-west slices, one beneath the other, each starting from the Mediterranean Sea (or, in the case of Zebulun and Gad, reaching the Sea via the "River of Egypt") and extending westward to the eastern border – however it is finally staked out.

Some Border Notes

From this table, and seeing how the tribes are arranged, several points are worth taking note of.

[139] Ezekiel 48:1-7 & 23-28.

- All the tribes are represented, except that Levi's lands are contained within the "Dedicated Region" (specifically, the Sacred District[140]) and perhaps, if the Prince so chooses, Levitical cities spread throughout the other provinces[141].

- All other tribes are represented in their own regions, just as in the original land assignments in Canaan. Note that contrary to certain Christian traditions, the tribe of Dan is very much alive and well in the Messianic era[142].

- The tribe of Joseph, as always, is split into (and "doubled" by) his sons Ephraim and Manasseh (47:13b), just as it has been since the Egyptian captivity.

- The total number of tribes therefore remains, technically, thirteen[143], though in some enumerations Ephraim and Manasseh are contracted into "Joseph" to keep the number representative of the twelve sons of Israel.

- Though widths are not given for each province, their north-to-south *order* is firm. Interestingly, the north-south order does *not* follow the original tribal allocations at all.

---

[140] Ezekiel 48:22, etc., in conformance with the land assignments after the original exodus.

[141] Following the pattern of the "Cities of Refuge" (Numbers 35; Joshus 20-21; 1 Chronicles 6), though presumably with a purpose different than protecting accidental killers.

[142] In the lack of mention of Dan in the list of Revelation 7:5-8, it has been opined that such is "due perhaps to Dan's early connection with idolatry (Jdg 18:30), or to a tradition that the antichrist was to come from that tribe" (footnote to Revelation 7:6, NIV Study Bible, Grand Rapids, MI: Zondervan Publishing House, 1995). Yet with the explicit inclusion of Dan in these times of Messiah, and as there are other explanations for why that tribe is not in the Revelation list (and especially since "antichrist" arises from a non-Israelite nation), such "traditions" lack Biblical support.

[143] There was never some sort of mystical European "thirteenth tribe" of Israel. Levi, even though "extracted" from Israel by the Lord (in exchange for all the firstborn of the nation – Numbers 3:41ff, 8:18), and therefore precluded from a distinct tribal land, always retained its full status of "tribe" nonetheless. In order to keep the number of tribal *lands* at twelve though, Joseph's tribe was divided into two. Thus there have *always* been, since the Egyptian captivity, thirteen tribes of Israel: with one of them being specially dedicated to and extracted by the Lord, and one other being blessed and doubled to fill the void.

- Each province shares the same borders to east and west; each has very straight borders above and below[144].

Allocation by Population

Once again, the provinces will not necessarily be equal in area. True, Ezekiel is ordered to divide the land "equally" among the tribes[145], but this does not mean that each province has an identical quantity of square kilometers. Rather, all citizens are to be *treated equally*[146] in this regard. Though not explicitly repeated in Ezekiel, the clear precedent here is when the tribal lands were first assigned in Canaan:

> *Unto these the land shall be divided for an inheritance according to the number of names. 54 To many thou shalt give the more inheritance, and to few thou shalt give the less inheritance: to every one shall his inheritance be given according to those that were numbered of him.*
> *Numbers 26:53-54, KJV*

Again, "inheritance" equals land in this context of tribal-territory allocation, whether the process takes place in ancient or future events. Three times in two verses, this form of "inheritance" is mentioned; so in its final administering, the principles here are worth paying attention to. And what is the basic principle? The larger-population tribes get more land.

We can expect therefore that the north-to-south widths of the provinces will vary, resulting in an area distribution that is proportional to internal population. Since we cannot know what those proportions will be, we cannot draw firm lines between one tribal province and the next. Only the coming Prince will have the knowledge and wisdom to take all such matters into account and make these determinations.

---

[144] Seen in the only north-south "provincial" dimension given (for the Prince's lands), a consistent 25,000 cubits in width, all the way across – Ezekiel 48:8.

[145] Ezekiel 47:13a, 48:29.

[146] The Hebrew phrase in Ezekiel 47:14 is *'iysh k^{a}'aachiyw*, that is, each man treated like his brother.

A Tentative Distribution

What is to be Allocated

But, it doesn't hurt to guess. So let's take our best shot, beginning with a refresh of overall borders as they have been discussed, and how they align with contemporary Israel. Limiting the "clean slate" to what is contained[147] within Millennial Israel, the next map attempts to illustrate the territory to be divided up and assigned.

[147] The northern and southern extensions have been argued to be vassal regions *not* contained in Israel, and are not shown.

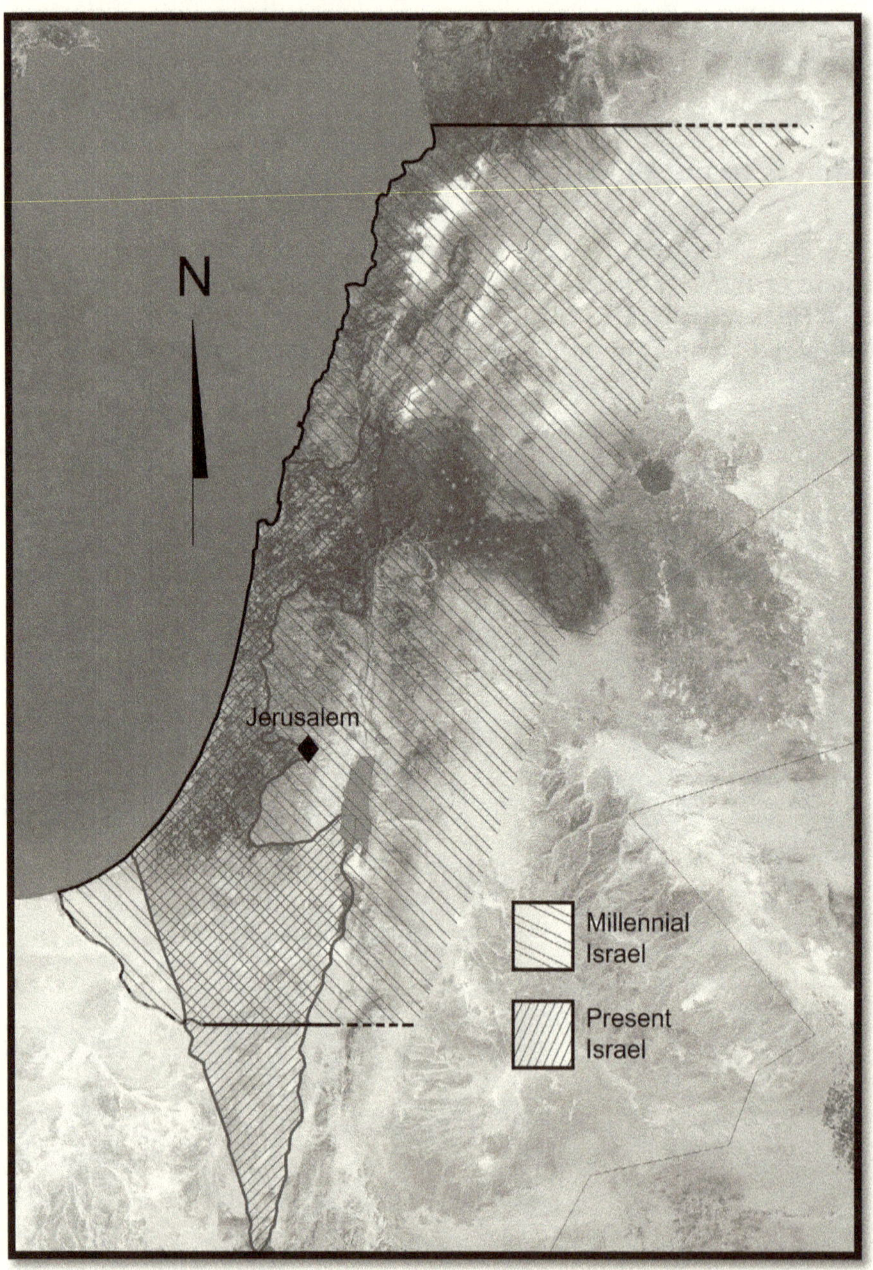

Figure 9: Area & Border Comparisons

Though Jerusalem is well in the southern half, it is comfortably surrounded by future-Israelite territory. Likewise, the Dedicated Region that is tied to Jerusalem will be "in the midst of" (different from "centered within") Israel's tribal provinces.

This Dedicated Region, east and west of Jerusalem, is unprecedented. It also acts as a geographic anchor for mapping, and a dividing line for the country's northern and southern portions. Seven tribes lie to the north and five to the south. Though not symmetric (as in a 6 north / 6 south split), it doesn't need to be; for the arrangement better divides the land amongst the provinces.

An Example Arrangement

With these points in mind, and also those of population distribution and prophesied arrangement, the following is an illustration of how the Lord might assign the Holy Land into its tribal provinces.

Judah has been much enlarged in this arrangement, and by an arbitrary amount; we can only guess. With respect to its comparatively large property needs, only the Lord will be able to decide how much Judah's borders will be adjusted. Likewise for all the other tribes, population will affect land allocations for each of the provinces, and those needs heave yet to be ascertained by the Prince.

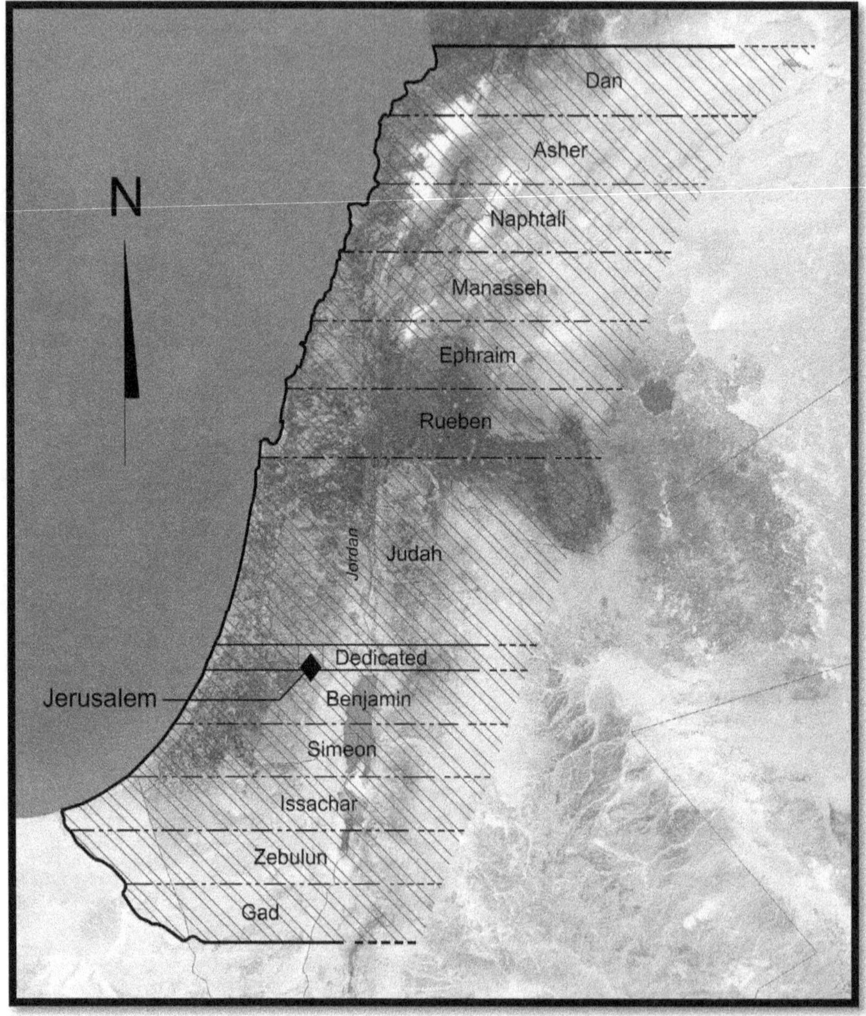

Figure 10: Distribution Possibilities

But for purposes of this survey, the region north of Judah is shown split into roughly equal areas for the six tribes there. Similarly, the area south of the Dedicated Region is shown divided into five approximately equal portions. Again, the actual proportions will vary from what is shown. When the Prince assesses all, He will make His wise and equitable decisions.

Chapter 5: Regional Color

And Jacob called unto his sons, and said, "Gather yourselves together, that I may tell you that which shall befall you in the last days."

Genesis 49:1, KJV

"...to sit at my right or left is not for me to grant. These places belong to those for whom they have been prepared by my Father."

Matt 20:20b, NIV

The Beautiful Landscape

Israel is a beautiful land today, and perhaps was even more so in ancient times when it was nicknamed "the land flowing with milk and honey[148]." In the Day of the Lord's rule it will be spectacular; and it will be, as in ancient times, apportioned to the twelve tribes. In this next leg of the journey we will look at what might make each tribal region special. But we will start with certain geographical features that all will enjoy.

Shared Elements

In ancient times, the tribal lands differed wildly in size and situation, with one being gigantic and another being tiny, one having coastal areas and the next not, and so on. Here it is almost the opposite, with many characteristics shared in common.

- **Ocean Access.** Except for Zebulun and Gad, all provinces start from the Mediterranean to the west. And even those two tribes border on the Wadi el-Arish which will presumably – because of enormous water flow through that channel[149] – permit maritime access to the Sea. Each tribe therefore has the potential of a major oceanic port.

- **Similar Cross Section.** Starting from the coast, each province stretches to the highlands in the east. In between are major features such as the coastal plains, foothills leading up to the central mountain range(s) and, just east of that, the Great Jordan Rift Valley. Keep in mind that the land will be smoothed out to at least some degree ("like the arabah," at least in the southern portion[150]). But it appears that each tribe will have this basic profile, or at least all of its elements represented.

---

[148] E.g., Exodus 3, 13, 33, etc.

[149] E.g., streams in prior wilderness areas (Isaiah 53:6), and from every high hill (Isaiah 30:25), with Judah being particularly blessed in this regard (Joel 3:18), the natural result being that these waters are aggregated into major features such as the "River of Egypt" cited here.

[150] Zechariah 14:10.

- **Elevated "Zion Range."** Perhaps the most prominent tectonic prophesy is that of Mount Zion being made "chief of the mountains[151]." Though many take this as a figurative statement, the many other prophecies that speak of related geographic events firmly argue this to be a literal, as well as a symbolic, phenomenon. So while other mountains may well be lowered by comparison[152], the Lord's Mountain will be visibly "exalted." Even so, the Judean Mountains are still present, as seen in many Millennial-era references to the mountains of Israel. Zion is part of this central north-to-south mountain range, so a natural assumption would be that the entire ridge is uplifted in the same tectonic event of Zion's. Each tribe will encounter this range; and each tribe's highest elevation will be at a point along it.

- **Highs and Lows.** Putting the above two points together, we see serious elevation changes enjoyed by all the tribes. The extreme height will be Mount Zion, while the extreme depth (at least currently) is the lowest place on the Earth, the Dead Sea, at 1360 feet (-414 m) below sea level[153]. Each tribe will share in this geographic diversity.

- **Lots of Water.** With the Lord's coming, numerous new streams will erupt into action, with every "high mountain" and "lofty hill" having water flowing nearby.[154]. The most important instances are the three new rivers arising from the Sacred District (a matter for later on). But with all ravines of Judah as a key example[155], most ravines of other provinces can also be expected to have a significant stream. Each tribe will share in this aquatic bounty.

- **The Royal Highway.** Of all the roads within Millennial Israel, the most important will be the King's Highway from Egypt to Assyria[156], travelling north-to-south through each of the provinces. Each tribe will share access to this most important road, and interact with domestic and international travelers upon it.

[151] Isaiah 2:2; Micah 4:1.

[152] See Habakkuk 3:6ff; Psalms 97:5; Nahum 1:5. In general, this massive event involves the whole land rising upward some, then relaxing back down (Amos 8:8), most likely as part of the Earth's most impressive quake in all human history (Revelation 16:18-20).

[153] Cited from the National Park Service web site article "Lowest Places on Earth, http://www.nps.gov/deva/naturescience/lowest-places-on-earth.htm.

[154] Isaiah 30:25.

[155] Joel 3:18.

[156] Isaiah 19:23.

- **Shared Discoveries.** One of the most intriguing prophecies is that the Israelites will be known as rebuilders of "ancient ruins", "Repairer of Broken Walls," "Restorer of Streets with Dwellings."[157] In all this archaeology and restoration, there will be remarkable discoveries related to Israel's colorful Biblical past. Each tribe will share in these many wonderful stories that come to the light of day, stories throughout the length and breadth of the Holy Land.

Regional Distinctions

Perhaps other geographic things come to your mind, for prophesied conditions shared by Israel's tribal provinces. Clearly, the above list is not the exhaustive last word in Biblical clues on the matter. Travelling forward though, we will next examine certain differences between provinces, and how they might be grouped into larger regions.

There are many ways to approach this task. If one wanted to do a really good job, many layers of knowledge come into play: ancient meanings, Biblical events, original territories, modern and ancient neighbors, geophysical technicalities, climatic and industrial differences, and so on. Clearly, we can only scratch the surface of story here. So we will use a different approach, one that speaks to why the tribes might be arranged as Ezekiel describes.

To that, we will look at the words spoken at the birth of each tribe's namesake, and at his paternal blessing. In other words, we will examine the words of mother and father, and see if they can shed some light for us.

Meet the Parents

As for the mothers of each of Israel's tribes, five women hold a claim; but ultimately, in the prophetic application, there are mainly two: Rachel (the beautiful one loved by Jacob[158]) and Leah (the eldest, shown the most favor by the Lord[159]). When Rachel got desperate over her barrenness, she gave her servant Bilhah to Jacob, to act as a surrogate and bear children *for Rachel*[160]. That worked; so Leah did the same thing, giving her servant Zilpah to Jacob[161].

[157] Isaiah 58:12.

[158] Genesis 29:16-18.

[159] Genesis 29:31-32, 30:17-18.

[160] Genesis 30:3.

[161] Genesis 30:9-11.

Eventually God helped Rachel, the result being two sons that became extremely blessed, so much so that her eldest, Joseph, became "split" into two full-fledged tribes. As discussed earlier, Jacob formally claimed Joseph's two sons as his own, which means that their grandmother Rachel effectively became their mother – in the legal order of things. The sons of Asenath (Joseph's wife), like those of Bilhah, therefore became the legally-reckoned and "direct" offspring of Rachel.

Though the ancient story about Rachel and Leah is one of competition in childbearing, and though we may be inclined to root for one over another, the fact is that the two are held in equal regard in the Biblical narrative. Both of them were very strong women, both worked hard for (seven years each) by Jacob-Israel, both were nieces of their mother-in-law Rebekah, both were massively blessed and honored by the Lord, and both received His divine assistance in childbearing. As we will see in the tribal distribution, the sons – however reckoned – of both women are equally favored.

It is in this light that we should take into account the naming of the sons, because the names were chosen with serious thought and emotion by these two women. At times, in fact, it seems that there was prophecy at work in the words of these two women, all those many years ago.

As for the father, there was only one: Jacob-Israel. His blessings will also be examined for each tribe; and like the mother's words are below quoted from Genesis (using the KJV). Note this though: when each son was blessed by the man Israel (Jacob), he uttered this puzzling prophecy:

> *And Jacob called unto his sons, and said, Gather yourselves together,* ***that I may tell you that which shall befall you in the last days.***
> *Genesis 49:1, KJV*

We are exploring the Holy Land of the "last days," the very land that Jacob was promised and concerned for; and we are interested in what "befalls" each of the tribes on those "last days." And though some of Jacob's statements applied to the historical circumstances, many of them find a final outcome in how the tribes are dispositioned under Messiah. Each of these tribes, even Manasseh and Ephraim[162], were Israel's sons, having an inheritance of territory. We will be travelling through their lands, as finally and ultimately established by God, and as sometimes hinted at by the mother and father in their parental blessings.

162 Upon his deathbed, Jacob claimed Joseph's two sons as his (just as if born directly to him like his first and second born sons), and blessed them as if his own: Genesis 48:5-20.

The Northern Region

Starting Points

This is the first of three "excursions" amongst the tribes, beginning with the less honored and travelling toward the most honored. "Honored" here means position, with respect to the Dedicated Region and the Sacred District within – where the Lord's throne will be. It will be a countdown of sorts, starting with the outer tribes and building towards the inner, taking the left hand (north) first, then the right hand (south)[163].

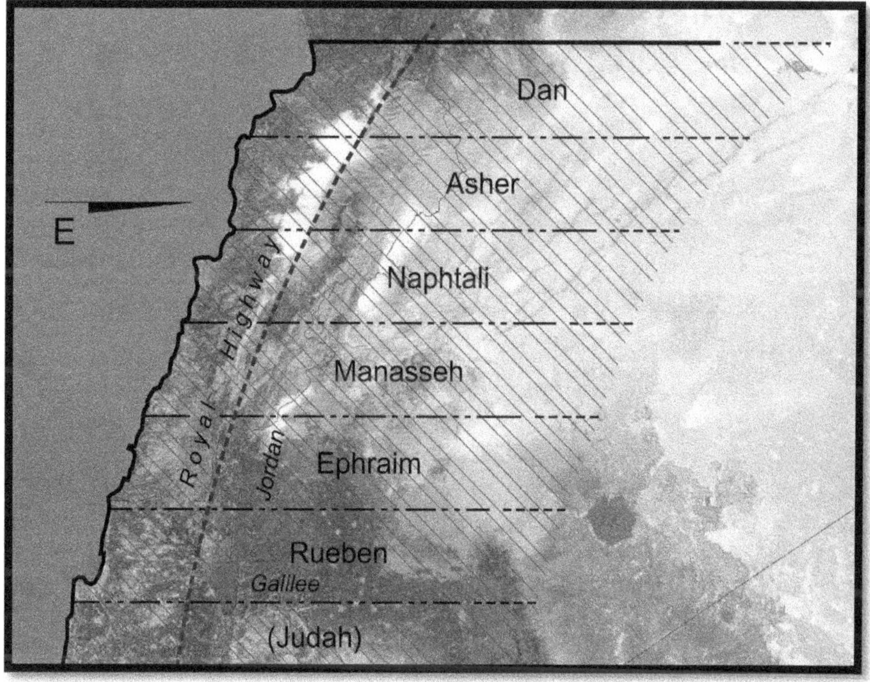

Figure 11: Northern Tribes

[163] Conceptually, with the Lord's Temple (within the Sacred District and Dedicated Region) facing east, His "left hand" is towards the north and His "right hand" is towards the south. The Hebrew word for "east," the cardinal direction, refers to the forward direction as one toward the sunrise. This is why the Hebrew word for "right" (*yamiyn,* Strong's 3225) can have the sense of "south" (e.g., 1 Samuel 23:19,24).

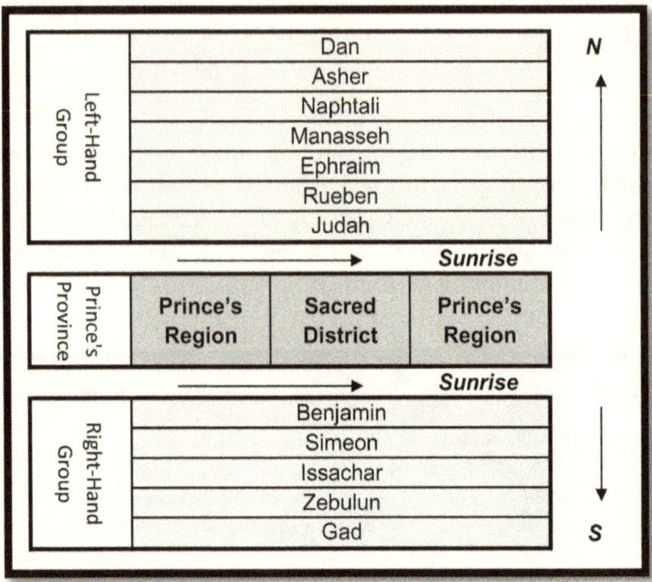

Figure 12: Left & Right Hand Positions

In the figurative sense, the northern tribes are located at God's left hand. By no means should this seem dishonored, but the opposite: to be near the King, even on His left, is vast honor indeed[164]. So we begin with the northern ("left hand") group, and northernmost tribe, Dan, heading south to Reuben. In a sense, we are following the Royal Highway from the northern border, travelling southward toward the most important provinces surrounding Messiah's Capital City, but stopping when we reach Judah's border.

164 See Matthew 20:21-23; Mark 10:37-40.

Dan

Birth Order:	**5**	Mother:	**Rachel (Bilhah)**	Meaning:	**"judge"**
Mother's Naming:	30:6	And Rachel said, God hath judged me, and hath also heard my voice, and hath given me a son: therefore called she his name **Dan**.			
Father's Blessing:	49:16 -17	**Dan** shall judge his people, as one of the tribes of Israel. 17 Dan shall be a serpent by the way, an adder in the path, that biteth the horse heels, so that his rider shall fall backward.			

Dan is located "on the left hand" of Jerusalem and the Temple, and farthest away from it. His mother was Bilhah, servant of Rachel, and this is where we first detect an important pattern. Like the other sons of surrogate mothers (Asher and Naphtali in the north, Gad in the south), Dan's position is furthest away from Jerusalem.

Taken with Jacob's odd "blessing" and the bad rap from a particular Christian tradition[165], one might think Dan's outermost and left hand position and status to be less than fortunate. But let's be clear: the tribe of Dan will flourish in the Lord's Day, having a full-fledged province assigned. Jacob's blessing should be seen as imbuing Dan's progeny with stealth and cunning in warfare – a very useful thing. Dan would indeed be known in this capacity[166], with the most famous Danite (and one of Israel's Judges) being the strongest man ever: Samson[167].

Dan was also one of the four leader-tribes during the initial exodus story, heading up three tribes to the north of the Tabernacle and camp[168]. Dan also led this same tribal threesome in travelling, as rear-guards for the nation[169].

---

[165] For not being listed in Revelation 7:4-8, as discussed earlier.

[166] Josh 19:47ff; Judges 18:1ff.

[167] Judges 13:2ff.

[168] Numbers 2:25-31.

[169] Numbers 10:25-28.

Who were the other tribes in these original exodus arrangements? The same as shown here: Asher, then Naphtali. Even in Moses' blessings upon the tribes, this group and order were kept[170]. As it was then, this same trio, and the same northern position, is being memorialized and preserved in the Prince's time.

North-South Order	Mother
Dan	Rachel (Bilhah)
Asher	Leah (Zilpah)
Naphtali	Rachel (Bilhah)
Joseph (Manasseh)	Rachel (Asenath)
Joseph (Ephraim)	Rachel (Asenath)
Rueben	Leah
Judah	Leah
Dedicated Reg. (Levi)	Leah
Benjamin	Rachel
Simeon	Leah
Issachar	Leah
Zebulun	Leah
Gad	Leah (Zilpah)

Figure 13: Tribal-Mother Positions

We will give the last word though to Rachel, Dan's legal mother, in her name assignment: "*judge*". As Jacob later said, Dan will indeed stand with all the other tribes, being represented in jurisprudence under the Prince[171]. Furthermore, for all those travelling from the north (including Europe and Asia), Dan will be the "greeter" and, in a sense, "gatekeeper" for the Royal Highway on the northern end. Since the gates of an ancient Biblical city were where the elders gathered to judge various matters[172], Dan can be described as one of the "guardian" positions, exercising "judgment" on behalf of all Israel.

170 Deuteronomy 33:22-24.

171 Perhaps seen in Revelation 11:16-17, 20:4.

172 E.g., Deuteronomy 21:19, 25:7; Proverbs 31:23.

Asher

Birth Order:	8	Mother:	**Leah (Zilpah)**	Meaning:	**"happy"**
Mother's Naming:	30:13	And Leah said, Happy am I, for the daughters will call me blessed: and she called his name **Asher**.			
Father's Blessing:	49:20	Out of **Asher** his bread shall be fat, and he shall yield royal dainties.			

As was just mentioned, Asher's tribe was associated with Dan (and Dan's brother Naphtali) from the very start. This is in spite of the fact that Asher was born of a very different mother (naturally and legally), and that his only "uterine" brother Gad is at the opposite end of the country.

However, when the Prince establishes His dominion here, Asher will have a lot to be happy about, keeping in mind that Jacob's blessings are ultimately fulfilled "in the last days." We see prophesied for Asher a lot of "bread," "fat," and "royal dainties." Moses' blessing was confirming: "*...let him dip his foot in oil.*"[173] Even in a time when the entire world will see the Lord's healing and prospering of creation, it sounds as if this province will be particularly blessed in its agriculture.

Naphtali

Birth Order:	6	Mother:	**Rachel (Bilhah)**	Meaning:	**"wrestling", or "I have wrestled"**
Mother's Naming:	30:8	And Rachel said, With great wrestlings have I wrestled with my sister, and I have prevailed: and she called his name **Naphtali**.			
Father's Blessing:	49:21	**Naphtali** is a hind let loose: he giveth goodly words.			

In a sense, food-producer Asher was grouped with, and between, two fighters. Full brother to Dan, Naphtali was prophesied to be like a dear ("hind"), because that animal perfectly symbolizes inexhaustible swiftness and nimbleness:

> *The Sovereign Lord is my strength; he makes my feet like the feet of a deer, he enables me to go on the heights.*
> *Habakkuk 3:19, NIV*

173 Deuteronomy 33:24b.

These attributes were seen as particularly helpful to the warrior[174], which Naphtali had plenty of[175]. Rachel's naming, "wrestler," was quite fitting.

In addition, this tribe was blessed to be good with words, or at least the ability to deliver good news. When applied in the Day to come, what will this mean? A fondness for lyrics and poetry, and perhaps the ability for their authoring? We can't be sure. However Naphtali's distinctions work out though, they will be plentiful. As Moses blessed the tribe, "*O Naphtali, satisfied with favour, and full with the blessing of the Lord*[176]..." And that is blessing indeed.

Let's pause for a little fork in the road. If a strict "order of honor" were to be followed, we would move next to Gad – in the southern region, and southernmost position. If you wish to keep with that order, please read that section next. Otherwise, we will complete the northern set first.

(Joseph)

Birth Order:	**11**	Mother:	**Rachel**	Meaning:	**"He will add"**
Mother's Naming:	30:24	And she called his name **Joseph**; and said, The Lord shall add to me another son.			
Father's Blessing (excerpts):	49:22-26	**Joseph** is a fruitful bough, even a fruitful bough by a well; whose branches run over the wall... 25b the Almighty, who shall bless thee with blessings of heaven above, blessings of the deep that lieth under, blessings of the breasts, and of the womb... 26b they shall be on the head of **Joseph**, and on the crown of the head of him that was separate from his brethren.			

Though not having a tribal province named after him, mention of Joseph must be made, for his story affects our understanding of his sons, and therefore their provinces.

There are so many interesting prophetic things going on with Joseph, beginning with his miraculously-enabled birth[177] and his name: for somehow, Rachel knew that she would be granted another son. And so she was, not only

[174] E.g., 2 Samuel 2:18; 1 Chronicles 12:8.
[175] E.g., the 10,000 who helped deliver Israel, under the direction of Deborah and Barak: Judges 4:6ff.
[176] Deuteronomy 33:23a, KJV.
[177] Genesis 30:22-23.

with Benjamin, but two more: the sons of Joseph, Manasseh and Ephraim, reckoned as Jacob's sons, and thus hers.

Jacob pulled out all the stops when he blessed Joseph, and Moses confirmed it[178]. The two tribes that represent Joseph are the recipients of the prophecies and promises of Jacob and Moses. In addition to any blessings that Manasseh or Ephraim received as individuals, the primary ones were those bestowed on their father, and were transmitted upon them.

Manasseh

Birth Order:	**11A**	Mother:	**Rachel (Asenath)**	*Meaning:*	**"cause to forget"**
Mother's Naming:	30:24	(see Joseph)			
Father's Blessing:	48:20	And he blessed them that day, saying, In thee shall Israel bless, saying, God make thee as Ephraim and as **Manasseh**: and he set Ephraim before **Manasseh**.			

Manasseh, the older, was deliberately seconded to Ephraim by Jacob. Accordingly, Manasseh is slightly less honored in position and therefore encountered next, just north ("left") of his younger brother. We are speaking of relative honoring: for both these tribes were fabulously blessed in history, with Manasseh needing two vast tracts of land (one on each side of the Jordan) to accommodate "his" progeny. Indeed, this tribe's growth was plentiful enough to make all Joseph's prior hardships "forgotten," which is what Manasseh means. And between the prophecy-blessings of Jacob and Moses, Manasseh (and Ephraim) "have it all."

But what will be this tribe's signature traits, the elements that might distinguish it from others in the Day of Yeshua's reign? True, the Lebanese region (contained by these northernmost tribes) will again enjoy arboreal restoration, and high lumber production[179]. Otherwise, we cannot really tell. But with his father's famous coat as a sign perhaps, we can know there will be many special blessings for Manasseh and his "younger" brother-tribe.

---

[178] Deuteronomy 33:13-17.

[179] Isaiah 60:13.

Ephraim

Birth Order:	**11B**	Mother:	**Rachel (Asenath)**	Meaning:	**"fruitfulness"**
Mother's Naming:	30:24	(see Joseph)			
Father's Blessing:	48:20	And he blessed them that day, saying, In thee shall Israel bless, saying, God make thee as **Ephraim** and as Manasseh: and he set **Ephraim** before Manasseh.			

Everything just said about Manasseh applies here to Ephraim, except to point out that the blessing was greater. Historically, the tribe became so predominant that the entire northern kingdom became known simply as "Ephraim[180]." This larger blessing conveys to our arrangement, where Ephraim again has the position more honored that Manasseh. Further, the Lord will still greatly value these two brother-tribes, as evidenced in this apocalyptic-era psalm:

> *God has spoken from his sanctuary: "In triumph I will parcel out Shechem and measure off the Valley of Succoth. 8 Gilead is mine,* ***Manasseh is mine; Ephraim is my helmet****, Judah my scepter.*
> *Psalms 108:7-8, NIV (also 60:6-7)*

Rueben

Birth Order:	**1**	Mother:	**Leah**	Meaning:	**"behold, a son"; or "He has seen my affliction."**
Mother's Naming:	29:32	And Leah conceived, and bare a son, and she called his name **Reuben**: for she said, Surely the Lord hath looked upon my affliction; now therefore my husband will love me.			
Father's Blessing:	49:3 -4	**Reuben**, thou art my firstborn, my might, and the beginning of my strength, the excellency of dignity, and the excellency of power: 4 Unstable as water, thou shalt not excel; because thou wentest up to thy father's bed; then defiledst thou it: he went up to my couch.			

[180] Vs. the southern kingdom which became named for its primary tribe, Judah.

The story of Reuben's downfall (referred to in Jacob's prophecy) is very sad. But though his actions led to forfeiture of his firstborn rights, the final story will see very good fortune for this tribe.

Though his name stemmed from Leah's sorrow over her rejection by Jacob, it stuck with Reuben nonetheless, applying to his affliction as well. God has seen the affliction of Reuben, throughout history, including that pertaining to the loss of firstborn honor. Of the northern tribes that border on the central trio, Reuben's is the closest, and therefore the most honored of the entire northern six.

The nation will indeed "behold" this "son," so long paying for the sins of the father, so long eclipsed by other tribes, but now in a place of prominence. As Moses declared, "*Let Reuben live, and not die; and let not his men be few.*"[181] Reuben will prosper greatly under the Prince; and whatever unique blessings He bestows on this province, they will surely be wonderful.

---

[181] Deuteronomy 33:6, KJV.

The Right Hand Region

Starting Points

Here begins our next excursion through Millennial tribal territories, now starting from the furthest one to the south. We will then work our way north toward the most central positions surrounding the King's City, Jerusalem, stopping when we get to Benjamin's border.

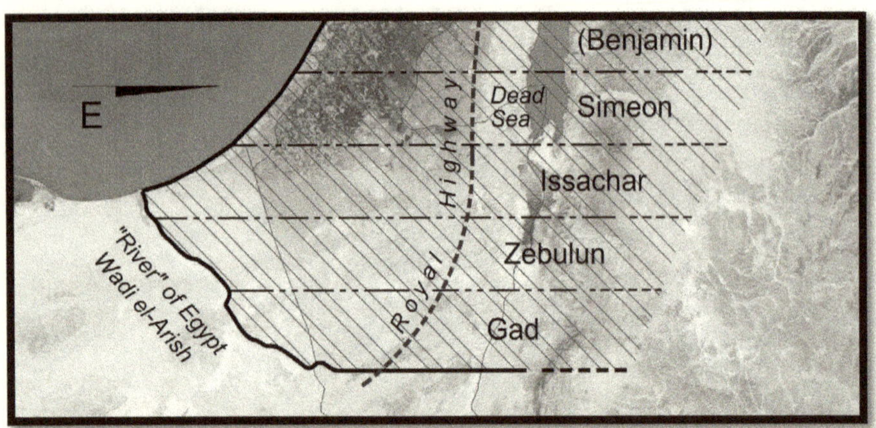

Figure 14: Southern Tribes

Earlier we discussed how Millennial water flow issues would cause Wadi el-Arish (and many other ravines) to be major, year-round water courses. As in no other time in history, this channel will truly be the "river" of Egypt, and will appear quite different than what is indicated on the above map. In addition to serving as the border between Egypt and Israel, this river will open upon the Mediterranean and (as argued prior) permit ship transportation thereto. This means that even the southernmost tribes have shipping access to western destinations: even Zebulun, which will finally have its long-prophesied "havens" for ships[182].

[182] Genesis 49:13.

As for the region in general, the further south one went, the more it was known for its dryness and inhospitableness. The term "negev" (or *negeb*) means "dry," and became synonymous for areas south of ancient Judah. Under Messiah's creative and restoring power, however, such regions will be made green with new rivers[183], particularly this southern area once known as "Judah"[184].

> *I will make rivers flow on barren heights, and springs within the valleys. I will turn the desert into pools of water, and the parched ground into springs. 19 I will put in the desert the cedar and the acacia, the myrtle and the olive. I will set pines in the wasteland, the fir and the cypress together, 20 so that people may see and know, may consider and understand, that the hand of the Lord has done this, that the Holy One of Israel has created it.*
> *Isaiah 41:18-20, NIV*

With that kind of water availability and botanic flourishing, the southland will no doubt become greatly inhabited. In fact, we are particularly informed that "*exiles from Jerusalem who are in Sepharad*"[185] in will settle here. Whether this refers to Sephardic Jews in general, or a more specific group, is for others to discern. Whoever they are, they will enjoy not wasteland and wilderness, but beautiful green lands that are well watered and full of trees and other forms of life.

---

[183] E.g., Isaiah 41:18.
[184] Joel 3:18.
[185] Obadiah 20, NIV.

Gad

Birth Order:	**7**	Mother:	**Leah (Zilpah)**	*Meaning:*	**"overcome"; or, "good fortune"**
Mother's Naming:	30:11	And Leah said, A troop cometh: and she called his name **Gad**.			
Father's Blessing:	49:19	**Gad**, a troop shall overcome him: but he shall overcome at the last.			

Gad, the full brother of Asher to the north, is named after the idea of pressing or overcoming by force, as with a military troop. Jacob's blessing was a play on his name, making it clear to us that ultimately, Gad would do the overcoming, in spite of being downtrodden in the past. Perhaps it was the Prince, Yeshua, who Moses referred to in his blessing over Gad: "*Blessed be he that enlargeth Gad…*"[186], for indeed, the Prince will cause this tribe's lands to be enlarged, and find "good fortune."

Regarding proximity to the King's City, the other southern tribes are more honored. However, there are a number of reasons why Gad has a special position of a different form, the kind of protective situation that the northernmost tribe will have. In Moses' blessing, Gad is described as a lion – as is Dan[187] (and Judah). Indeed, some of Gad's warriors had faces that seemed like those of lions[188], at least in ferocity. Also like Dan, Gad is the southern "gateway" tribe: foreigners entering the Royal Highway from the south must pass through him. In connection with this "gatekeeper" role, just like Dan, Gad is also associated with the function of "judge" by Moses:

> *And he provided the first part for himself, because* ***there, in a portion of the lawgiver, was he seated;*** *and he came with the heads of the people, he executed the justice of the Lord, and his judgments with Israel.*
> *Deuteronomy 33:21, KJV*

The north and south tribes are therefore *both* strong, lion-like "gatekeepers" for tomorrow's Israel, *both* having a judge-like role in this regard. Though both these tribes are the furthest from the King's City, they have the special distinction of being His trusted border-keepers to north and south. And when people come from other nations, taking an overland route, it will most likely be one of these two tribes that they first encounter in Israel.

---

186 Deuteronomy 33:20b, KJV.
187 Deuteronomy 33:22.
188 1 Chronicles 12:8.

Zebulun

Birth Order:	**10**	Mother:	**Leah**	Meaning:	**"dwell with"**
Mother's Naming:	30:20	And Leah said, God hath endued me with a good dowry; now will my husband dwell with me, because I have born him six sons: and she called his name **Zebulun**.			
Father's Blessing:	49:13	**Zebulun** shall dwell at the haven of the sea; and he shall be for an haven of ships; and his border shall be unto Zidon.			

Named for Leah's forlorn hope to dwell more with his father, Zebulun's name refers to "habitation" or "dwelling place" in general. Jacob made an oblique play on this, but prophesying something seemingly random: Zebulun would be a "haven" for ships. This is odd, because not only is this a very explicit statement, but the tribal territory was land-locked[189]. If his border was intended to reach Sidon, or any coastline at all, it appears that this potential was never fulfilled in history.

However, we are speaking of times yet to come, "the last days" in which Jacob's prophesies find their ultimate application. Zebulun will, some day, be a place known for its harbors. The Wadi el-Arish, as argued before, will be flooded by new outflow from the north and east. If these prophesies are taken together and at face value, Zebulun's west "coast" will enjoy water flow and depth sufficient for deep water ports. In comparison with ports of other provinces (except Gad), Zebulon's will indeed be protected havens for ships, due to their being inland – like San Francisco or Baltimore.

What about "Sidon"? For Jacob's prophecy said Zebulun's border would reach that ancient location. Sidon is far to the north, and -- depending on where final borders are laid – will fall within perhaps Manasseh or Naphtali, far to the north. Yet Zebulun will now be way to the south, far from that ancient site, a seeming contradiction. But perhaps this element of Jacob's blessing applied to the ancient situation, and a potential for Zebulun that was never acquired.

There are other explanations though. If we take the phrase "*his border shall be unto*" to mean shipping reach and influence, this tribe's ships may well reach Sidon and other far-flung ports in Messiah's Day. Or, if "Sidon" was meant not by Jacob as a proper noun but the literal term "fishery[190]," Zebulon will indeed have tremendous fishing areas. Regardless, this province will apparently be

[189] E.g., International Standard Bible Encyclopedia; The Moody Atlas of Bible Lands; others.

[190] Strong's OT:6721, *tsiydown*. Sidon's modern name in Arabic is *Sayda* or *Saydoon*, in English *Saida*, located in Lebanon.

remarkable amongst the twelve for its maritime activities in the Prince's dominion.

North-South Order	Mother
Joseph (Manasseh)	Rachel (Asenath)
Joseph (Ephraim)	Rachel (Asenath)
Rueben	Leah
Judah	Leah
Dedicated Reg. (Levi)	Leah
Benjamin	Rachel
Simeon	Leah
Issachar	Leah
Zebulun	Leah

Figure 15: Positions of the "Direct" Sons

As for position of honor on the south side of Jerusalem, Zebulun is the first of the "direct" sons – that is, those actually born to either Rachel or Leah. If we take a tiny side trip and focus on only those tribes for the moment, we find further clues in the pattern of how the Lord arranged the tribes. Being natural mothers (not surrogate), and those that Jacob actually worked for fourteen years to marry, Rachel and Leah have position of prominence, and their biological sons do as well[191]. This is the clear pattern we see, for all these "direct" sons are clustered around the Prince's lands: three in the center, three on the left hand, and three on the right. We have already discussed those to the north. And with Zebulun, we have the first "direct" son on the "right hand."

Does any of this take away from the lot of Dan, Asher, Naphtali or Gad, as future tribal lands? Of course not, for we have seen them to have many blessings and honors already. Rather, we should appreciate that the Lord will grant greater honor where it is fitting, and that He never forgets His promises – no matter how long ago they were made.

[191] Including Joseph of course, with his two sons (Manasseh and Ephraim) being the doubling of his inheritance, and also being claimed by Jacob as his own natural sons.

Issachar

Birth Order:	**9**	Mother:	**Leah**	Meaning:	**"man [who] works," "man [who] earns"**
Mother's Naming:	30:18	18 And Leah said, God hath given me my hire, because I have given my maiden to my husband: and she called his name **Issachar**.			
Father's Blessing:	49:14 -15	**Issachar** is a strong ass couching down between two burdens: 15 And he saw that rest was good, and the land that it was pleasant; and bowed his shoulder to bear, and became a servant unto tribute.			

Seeing what Rachel had been doing, and concerned that she was past childbearing, Leah gave her servant Zilpah to Jacob as a potential surrogate mother. The result was Gad. But later, God helped Leah to start bearing again with this son. Thus the name Issachar: as far as the mother was concerned, "wages" for giving Zilpah to Jacob. Not the most complimentary of names! Yet as with other tribal names, the mothers' initial birth-competition is not always the final factor.

Issachar's name further evokes ideas of a hard worker and wage earner, and this is how Jacob applied that name in his blessing. Though having been a "*servant to tribute*" (KJV) or "*submit[ted] to forced labor*" (NIV), this "strong donkey" who bore many great burdens will find his place of rest under Messiah's rule, and see that it is good and pleasant. Though agriculture will be plentiful in that time to come, the work of the tribes will be voluntary and vigorous, not forced and wearying. The imagery coincides perfectly with something the Prince taught long ago:

> *"Come to Me, all who are weary and heavy-laden, and I will give you rest. 29 "Take My yoke upon you, and learn from Me, for I am gentle and humble in heart; and you shall find rest for your souls. 30 "For My yoke is easy, and My load is light."*
> *Matthew 11:28-30, NASB*

If any tribe needs rest, Issachar is apparently at or near the top of the list, for reasons known to God. In ancient times though, Issachar had a neighbor in similar circumstances of territory: Zebulun, who we just talked about. These two tribes, both descended from Leah's later two sons, held lands that were small and land-locked in the far north. Under the Prince's rule though, they will be neighbors once again, but in the southern region, and with spacious lands. Moses blessed them in the same breath:

> *And of Zebulun he said,* **Rejoice, Zebulun, in thy going out; and, Issachar, in thy tents.** *19 They shall call the people unto the mountain; there they shall offer sacrifices of righteousness: for they shall suck of the abundance of the seas, and of treasures hid in the sand.*
> *Deuteronomy 33:18-19*

In the past, neither tribe had access to the Sea. But under Messiah, Moses' blessing will be fulfilled: their lands will be as broad as all the others, spanning from the western Sea to the eastern highlands. They will enjoy the "*abundance of the seas,*" and the "*treasures hid in the sand.*" Zebulun will tend toward "going out" in ships; his slightly older brother will emphasize his dwelling places. And what sort of hidden treasures will these peoples uncover? Only the Lord knows – at least for now.

Simeon

Birth Order:	2	Mother:	**Leah**	Meaning:	**"to hear", or "hearing"**
Mother's Naming:	29:33	And she conceived again, and bare a son; and said, Because the Lord hath heard that I was hated, he hath therefore given me this son also: and she called his name **Simeon**.			
Father's Blessing:	49:5 -7	**Simeon** and Levi are brethren; instruments of cruelty are in their habitations. 6 O my soul, come not thou into their secret; unto their assembly, mine honour, be not thou united: for in their anger they slew a man, and in their selfwill they digged down a wall. 7 Cursed be their anger, for it was fierce; and their wrath, for it was cruel: I will divide them in Jacob, and scatter them in Israel.			

Let's be clear on why Judah became so prominent: because the first three sons, in Jacob's mind at least, disqualified themselves as leaders of what he knew would become a strong nation[192]. We have discussed Reuben, and have seen his province in an important northern position. Now we come to the second-born, Simeon. Jacob's "blessing" upon him (and Levi, the third-born) is chilling: to not be blessed at all by the father is a frightful thing, to be distanced and even cursed by him vastly worse.

---

192 In view of God's promises to Abraham, Isaac and himself, Israel.

Here's the brief story. A Canaanite clan wanted to intermarry with Jacob's family, and Jacob was willing. But when his daughter Dinah was raped, her brothers Simeon and Levi took vengeance – and slaughtered the entire clan when they were healing up from circumcision[193]. Jacob was furious, and – from his "blessing" – withdrew from these sons thereafter. Perhaps this is why Simeon is the only tribe not mentioned at all in Moses' blessings over the tribes just before his death.

Though just as culpable, Levi's tribe was later claimed by God for His own, as will be discussed later. But Levi's older brother, having been shamed by Jacob, was also for some reason ignored by Moses – who even gave the fallen firstborn, Reuben, at least some positive acknowledgement. The second-born, Simeon, did not receive even that. Things don't look good for the second-born son of Jacob.

The final word does not, however, belong to Jacob; and Moses' blessings did by no means exhaust the love and mercy of God Almighty. For what do we see of the other "errant brother," Levi? His tribe was elevated to the most honored position of service, extracted from all the tribes of Israel for God's purposes[194]. And what did we see for Reuben, the fallen first-born? The closest and most honored "left-hand" position thus far.

For Simeon, to be named for being "heard by the Lord" by the mother is a wonderful and very prophetic thing. This tribe will reside opposite Reuben, at the "right hand" of the core inner provinces, the most honored next to them. Is cases like Simeon's, one is reminded by the Prince's prophecy: "*…the last shall be first.*"[195]

---

[193] Genesis 34.

[194] E.g., Deuteronomy 18:1-2; Joshua 13:14.

[195] E.g., Matthew 20:16.

The Central Region

Starting Points

The three central provinces are honored above all the others. The Prince's province, enveloping the Sacred District, is the most honored: this is where Messiah Yeshua will have His throne, where Jerusalem will reside, and where the Temple will be. The positions on the immediate left (north) and right (south) of this province are also hugely important, as He more than hinted at long ago:

> *"...to sit at my right or left is not for me to grant. These places belong to those for whom they have been prepared by my Father."*
> *Matt 20:20b, NIV (see also Mark 10:40)*

As for what *individuals* are granted those honors, only the Father knows. But on the tribe-province-level we see precisely what the Father's decision has been: Judah on the left, and Benjamin on the right.

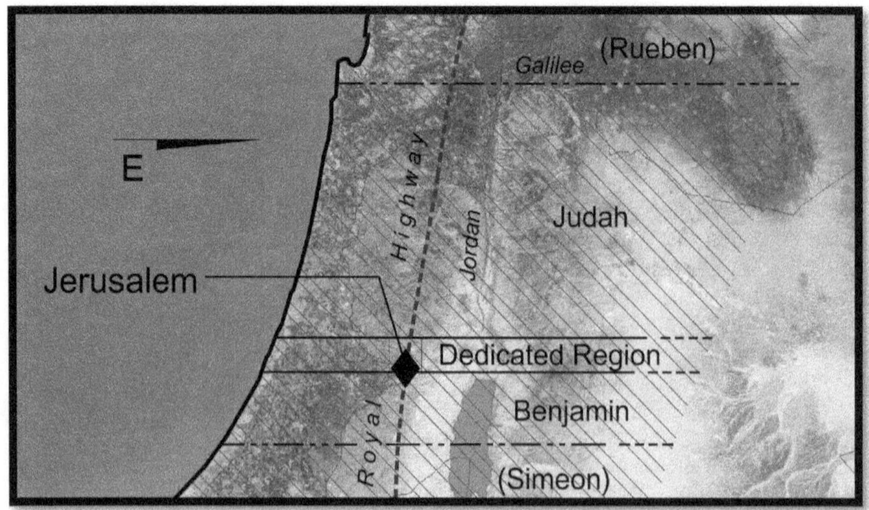

Figure 16: Central Tribes

These are the greatest three; and we now commence our final excursion amongst Israel's coming tribal provinces.

Judah

Birth Order:	**4**	Mother:	**Leah**	Meaning:	**"praised," "celebrated"**
Mother's Naming:	29:35	And she conceived again, and bare a son: and she said, Now will I praise the Lord: therefore she called his name **Judah**; and left bearing.			
Father's Blessing (excerpts):	49:8 -12	**Judah**, thou art he whom thy brethren shall praise: thy hand shall be in the neck of thine enemies; thy father's children shall bow down before thee. 9 Judah is a lion's whelp…10 The sceptre shall not depart from Judah, nor a lawgiver from between his feet, until Shiloh come; and unto him shall the gathering of the people be... 11b he washed his garments in wine, and his clothes in the blood of grapes: 12 His eyes shall be red with wine, and his teeth white with milk.			

As we see throughout the Bible, Judah has been – and will be – the most "praised" and "celebrated" of all the tribes, his leadership role continuing to find fulfillment in the Son of David, Yeshua. Of all Leah's naming-prophecies, unwitting or not, this is the greatest.

Judah's foremost position is equivalent with the status of firstborn son. Reuben forfeited those rights with his incest with his step mother. Simeon and Levi were passed over, because of their cruelty at Shechem. Being the next in line, fourth-born, Judah received – and retains – the position and rights of the firstborn.

In Chapter 6, we discussed Judah's prominence in Messiah's Day. And though many more things can be said, we will here mention his fittingly honored position with the Prince: directly next to Him, at His "left hand."

Benjamin

Birth Order:	12	Mother:	Rachel	Meaning:	"son of the right hand"
Mother's Naming:	35:17 -18	And as she was having great difficulty in childbirth, the midwife said to her, "Don't be afraid, for you have another son." 18 As she breathed her last — for she was dying — she named her son Ben-Oni. But his father named him **Benjamin**.			
Father's Blessing:	49:27 -28	**Benjamin** shall ravin as a wolf: in the morning he shall devour the prey, and at night he shall divide the spoil.			

At last, we come to the most honored tribal province, immediately next to the Prince's land but on the south side: the province of Benjamin. As a baby, the name his dying mother gave him was Ben-Oni: *son of sorrow*. Unlike all the other sons though, Jacob actually stepped in and gave the baby a different name: son (*ben*) + right [hand] (*yamiyn*), *Benjamin*. This name was the only one given to any of the sons by their father, a big prophetic flag in itself. For ultimately, Benjamin's lands will reside at the right hand of the Lord's.

Like the coastlands of adjacent tribes, Benjamin's will be known for its pasturelands that support sheep-raising[196]. With other tribes situated across what was anciently the territory of Judah, Benjamin will enjoy particular abundance in streams and rivers[197].

The most important thing though remains this most honored position. But other than the name, why would Benjamin have this "seat"? After all, he was the *last*-born, the *least* likely to gain such adulation. In fact, this was the tribe that fell into such idolatry and other abominations that it was virtually wiped out in consequence: not by a foreign country, but by the other tribes of Israel. Benjamin shouldn't have even survived as a tribe; but by God's grace, "he" did[198].

With the story of Benjamin, and that tribe's highest position of honor, we are reminded loudly of God's forgiveness. We are also strongly reminded again of something the Lord said on more than one occasion: that the last would be first[199]. This place of honor will be occupied by the last-born and least likely, all in praise of the Lord's mighty redemption of any of us. For in a sense, we are all Benjamin.

---

196 Ashkelon (falling most likely within Benjamin's prophesied territory) will, like other areas anciently held by Philistines, be known for this: Zephaniah 2:6-7.

197 Joel 3:18.

198 Judges 20-21.

199 Matthew 19:30, 20:16. Also Mark 9:35, 10:31; Luke 13:30.

Levi

Birth Order:	**3**	Mother:	**Leah**	Meaning:	**"attached", "joined to"**
Mother's Naming:	29:34	And she conceived again, and bare a son; and said, Now this time will my husband be joined unto me, because I have born him three sons: therefore was his name called **Levi**.			
Father's Blessing:	49:5-7	Simeon and **Levi** are brethren; instruments of cruelty are in their habitations… (see Simeon)			

Just as with the original obtaining of the Promised Land, the tribe of Levi has no province of "his" own in the coming dominion, because God withdrew this tribe for Himself in exchange for all the firstborn of Israel[200]. From Ezekiel's information, Levi's lands will be contained within the Sacred District. This is why his name is listed here in parentheses. Nevertheless, Levi remains a full-fledged tribe of Israel, and requires mention amongst his brethren here.

Like his full brother Simeon, Levi was rejected by Jacob. But as a tribe, Levi's was one chosen by God. Leah's naming was therefore again prophetic: for Levi was indeed "joined to" the Lord, in exclusive service to Him. And once again, under the final Joshua, Levi will enjoy an "attached" position to the Lord and His purposes, all within the Prince's province and Dedicated Region.

---

[200] E.g., Numbers 3:11ff.

Chapter 6: Princely Inheritance

And the Word became flesh and dwelt among us, and we beheld His glory, the glory as of the only begotten of the Father, full of grace and truth.

John 1:14, NKJV

"My dwelling place also will be with them; and I will be their God, and they will be My people."

Ezekiel 37:27, NASU

"...its length from east to west will equal one of the tribal portions; the sanctuary will be in the center of it."

Ezekiel 48:8b, NIV

A Puzzling Strip of Land

In ancient Israel, when determining a sacred district and a special the location of the Temple (the "place of His Name"), God chose a locale within one of the tribal portions. Specifically, the tribe so honored was the ruling tribe of Judah; and within that, King David's city, Jerusalem. What God did *not* do back then was to set aside a set-aside region of the country for His special purposes, but instead chose to have His Temple reside in the midst of His people, within the province of the foremost tribe.

In times ahead though, things will be very different. Some two-and-a-half millennia ago, God revealed to Ezekiel that in Messiah's coming kingdom, Israel would have an unprecedented feature: a huge strip of land that splits the country practically in two, as prominent in size as the other tribal provinces.

> *Bordering the territory of Judah from east to west will be the portion you are to present as a special gift. It will be 25,000 cubits wide, and its length from east to west will equal one of the tribal portions; the sanctuary will be in the center of it.*
> *Ezekiel 48:8, NIV*

But why this difference? When Messiah comes to reign, why would the Lord set aside such a dedicated region, distinct from Judah's or any other tribe's lands? Why would this area, from east to west, cut across the country as Ezekiel describes? And since Ezekiel says that the bulk of this region is especially dedicated to the Prince Himself, what might He do with such a vast amount of real estate?

Mysterious matters indeed! But the Lord has not left us without clues to these puzzles. In fact, He invites us to explore them[201]. Thus we embark on our next leg of the journey: an in-depth assessment of the borders and dimensions of this fascinating, and most important, "province" of Israel on the horizon.

---

[201] E.g., 2 Timothy 3:16.

His Place of Dwelling

An Emphatic Statement

Situated amongst the provinces, though narrow-ish, this prominent slice of land spans the land from the sea eastward. Appearing just like one of the tribal regions, it is almost as if the Lord Himself were making a gigantic statement: that His own dwelling place is not only again in the midst of His people on Earth, but now with just as much substance, vitality and legal authority as any of the other sons of Israel.

This concept of God's "tenting" amongst His people[202] is as ancient as the Exodus story, for that was the essential concept behind the holy Tabernacle ("tent"): *"Then have them make a sanctuary for me, and I will* ***dwell among them****"* (Exodus 25:8). This key idea was applied to Jesus' physical presence on Earth as well:

> *"And the Word became flesh and* **dwelt** *["tented"[203]]* **among us***, and we beheld His glory, the glory as of the only begotten of the Father, full of grace and truth."*
> *John 1:14, NKJV*

Such is one of the great themes of the Bible: an intimate relationship with God, fundamentally spiritual, but nonetheless expressed in physical and spatial nearness. With the arrangement of the ancient Temple within Jerusalem, and the setting of the Tabernacle amongst the tribal encampments, this objective of God's to completely *dwell* with His people is vibrantly displayed. Observe how strongly the Lord expresses Himself on this point:

> *When they [Israel] placed their threshold next to my [the Lord's] threshold and their doorposts beside my doorposts, with only a wall between me and them…*
> *Ezekiel 43:8a, NIV*

This was more than mere imagery: for the doors to God's Tabernacle and (later) Temple were truly within a short walking distance of Israelite doorways. But the first-chosen nation rebelled against the Lord, exemplifying that all peoples have gone wildly astray and fallen short of His glory[204]. And for two

---

[202] E.g., Exodus 25:8, 29:45-46; Numbers 5:3, 35:34.

[203] In Greek, *skenoo* (Strong's NT:4637).

[204] E.g., Isaiah 53:6; Romans 3:23.

thousand years, the *physical* "tenting" of the Lord among His people, by way of His Temple, has been materially absent.

The Coming "Tenting"

But a time is soon to come when this profound phenomenon will again take form on Earth: for the Lord will cause His Temple to be built anew. The special Presence of the Father will once more dwell therein; and Messiah, Son of God and Son of David, will personally dwell amongst His people in robust interaction.

Unlike the pre-exilic times in which Ezekiel's pronouncement above was made, there will be neither cause for offense to God's holiness, nor neglect in responsiveness to His loving supremacy: for His people will serve Him with all their being[205].

With this renewed form of intimacy will come an enhanced manifestation in the Lord's "tenting" amongst His people. In contrast with a Tabernacle moving with the tribal camps, or even a fixed Temple residing within the borders of a particular tribe (Judah), Ezekiel describes an *entire tribe-sized region* dedicated exclusively to the Lord Almighty. Specifically, this land will belong to The Anointed (*ha Mashiach*), the long-awaited Prince-King. For as has been prophesied for this time to come:

> *"**My dwelling place** ["tent" or "tabernacle"] **also will be with them**; and I will be their God, and they will be My people."*
> *Ezekiel 37:27, NASU*

> *For unto us a child is born, unto us a son is given: and **the government shall be upon his shoulder**: and his name shall be called Wonderful, Counsellor, The **mighty God**, The everlasting Father, The **Prince of Peace.***
> *Isaiah 9:6, KJV*

In times yet to come, this physical "dwelling" of God with humankind will have its most profound expression yet. Set amongst Israel's tribal areas, as in the wilderness journey, the Dedicated Region speaks both to the Lord's fulfillment of His promises to Abraham and his offspring, and His "tabernacling" amongst not only Israel's people, but *all* the nations[206].

---

[205] E.g., Leviticus 26:38-45; Deuteronomy 30:1-10; Jeremiah 31:31-37.

[206] Per Deuteronomy 32:8: when God divided mankind into the original nations (see Genesis 10), it was with an eye to how He chose to subdivide His first-chosen nation into its twelve tribes.

No longer satisfied with a small portion of property set within a certain tribal region, the Lord and Prince will have His own province set amongst those of the tribes. It is almost as if God will be the "neighbor" of Jacob's sons[207], in a lasting and very emphatic outworking. And since the Dedicated Region is comprised mostly of lands deeded to the Prince, it is *as if He Himself is a brother to Jacob's sons*, being *given an equal share of the land with them.*

Emanuel[208] will not only physically dwell with us again, but do so with all the intimacy seen in the Exodus arrangement, and with the royal and very physical presence of David and Solomon. He will dwell amongst all the tribes, with personal and ongoing relationship with His people as His brothers and sisters.

> *For whosoever shall do the will of God, the same is my brother, and my sister, and mother.*
> *Mark 3:35, KJV*

The Prince's Claims

Here is another question. Why are the Prince's properties not contained within Jerusalem or the Sacred District? One answer begins with the fact that Messiah, Son of God and King of Kings, is also the Son of (King) David and the direct heir to David's rights and authority. Though Jesus' anointing (*mashiach*) as *priest* is understandably emphasized[209] by Christians, He also bears the *kingly* anointing as well: as the promised Son of David, the great Prince to come.

From this royal inheritance perspective, we can appreciate why special lands will belong to Messiah when He comes into full possession of His kingdom on earth. Like His father David, He will have been a mighty warrior[210] and will receive his own lands in rightful honor of, and reward for, his deliverance after a period of battle and conquest[211]. Lands would be set aside

---

[207] See Ezekiel 43:8-9.

[208] Meaning "God with us": Isaiah 7:14, 8:8; Matthew 1:23.

[209] E.g., with respect to His atoning means and redemptive purposes, as seen in Isaiah 53, the Gospels, and elsewhere; doctrinally expounded upon in Hebrews chapters 2-10, supported by the numerous Scriptures quoted therein.

[210] Inherent in many of the prophecies that Messiah will come and redeem-rescue His people; an expectation held by Jesus' own disciples; a divinely spoken foreshadowing being via Cyrus the Great (Isaiah 44-45), also an explicit fact in John's visions of Armageddon (e.g., Revelation 19).

[211] Seen, for example, in the inheritances of Caleb and Joshua; and reflected in the vast lands owned by Solomon.

nearby for His personal use[212]. And if the reward is on any par with the magnificent salvation wrought by the Lord and King, these lands will be very large indeed – far too large to fit within the City.

Points to Ponder

Here are some points to consider in regards to Messiah's coming fulfillment of His role as David's Son.

- That He will indeed come and physically reign on this earth[213].
- That He as the Anointed (*mashiach,* Messiah) Prince will come in the role of warrior-King, in the same spirit and enablement of His natural father, David[214].
- That He will re-establish and confirm the physical kingdom of David[215].
- That His dominion will be both local (as Prince of Israel, Son of David) and global (as King of all kings[216]).
- That Messiah will receive, as the royal Son of David, his own lands in the midst of Israel's tribal provinces.
- That Messiah will make a "gift"[217] of his land for the Sacred District in accordance with his natural father's actions[218], and do so as personal representative of Israel[219].

---

[212] These awards of lands could also to be seen as God's remedy of Jesus' homeless status during His priestly ministry (see Matthew 8:20, Luke 9:58).
[213] Matthew 6:10; Luke 11:2; explicit in innumerable First Testament prophecies.
[214] As with all references in both First and New Testaments to the prophesied "Son of David." See Isaiah 63 and Revelation 19 for examples of the "warrior" element.
[215] E.g., Isaiah 9:6-7.
[216] 1 Timothy 6:15; Revelation 17:14, 19:16.
[217] Ezekiel 48:8.
[218] 2 Samuel 24:24; Chronicles 21:24.
[219] See Isaiah 49, in which Messiah is equated with the nation He represents: "*You are my servant, Israel, in whom I will display my splendor.*"

Mapping the Dedicated Land

Having understood at least some of the "why's" of this province, we can begin with the "what's" and "how's" of it. We are now at the very heart of the prophesied country, the Holy Land to come. We are within the set-aside region that contains not only the Prince's lands, but also the Capitol City and the Holy Temple. This is the *King's land* – that which He will hold legal and literal title to, and utilize for His regal purposes. And thanks to many clues in Scripture, we can now survey it.

Three Unique Indicators

Of the all the provincial regions described by Ezekiel, this special portion of land is dimensionally unique. For unlike the tribal provinces,

- ☐ Only the Dedicated "province" is described with a north-to-south dimension. *We are shown exactly how wide it will be.*

- ☐ Only the Dedicated "province" is prophetically described as divided into sub-sections. *We are shown exactly how it is internally arranged.*

- ☐ Only the Dedicated "province" has a specific anchor point. *We are shown exactly where it will be positioned, north-to-south.*

As for the first point, we are informed that the Dedicated Region is 25,000 ("long" or royal) cubits in north-to-south width[220]. This dimension converts to 8.15 miles, or 13.1 kilometers, applying all along its east-west length.

---

220 Ezekiel 48:8. See Appendix A: Royal Measuring Device for further background on the royal cubit employed here.

Three Distinct Sections

To the second point, unlike the other provinces, this one is subdivided into three specific sections. Near the center is the Sacred District[221] that measures 25,000 royal cubits (8.15 miles / 13.1 km) square. To east and west of it are the twin regions belonging to the Prince:

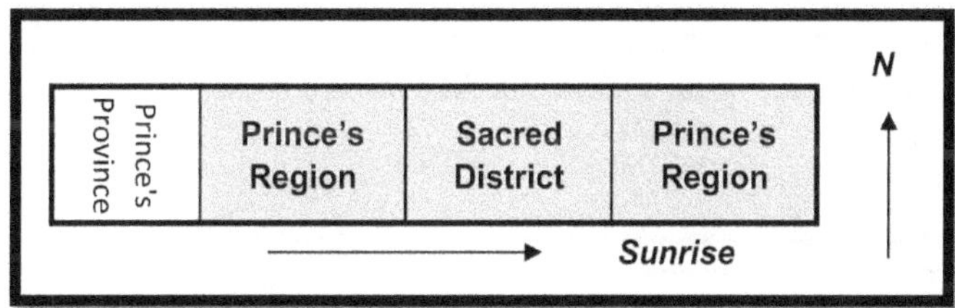

Figure 17: Sub-Divisions of the Prince's Province

> ***The prince will have the land bordering each side of the area formed by the sacred district and the property of the city.*** *It will extend westward from the west side and eastward from the east side, running lengthwise from the western to the eastern border parallel to one of the tribal portions.*
> *Ezekiel 45:7, NIV*

> *And beside the border of Judah, from the east side to the west side, shall be the allotment which you shall set apart, 25,000 cubits in width, and in length like one of the portions, from the east side to the west side; and the sanctuary shall be in the middle of it.*
> *Ezekiel 48:8, NASU*

> *So the property of the Levites*[222] *and the property of the city will lie* ***in the center*** *[that is, along the east-west axis] of* ***the area that belongs to the prince.*** *The area belonging to the prince will lie between the border of Judah and the border of Benjamin.*
> *Ezekiel 48:22, NIV*

---

[221] Ezekiel 45:1-7 and 48:8-20.

[222] That is, the larger sub-divisions of the Sacred District. The tribe of Levi, from which the priesthood originates, embraces both the Zadokite (priestly) and non-Zadokite (Levitical) subdivisions of the Sacred District.

The Prince's Province therefore resides in the midst of the tribal provinces, and the Sacred District lies in the midst of *that.*

Vertical Anchoring

The third unique indicator for this province is a particular feature within that serves as a north-to-south anchor point. Since we can know where it is within the province, its north and south borders can be placed with fair precision. As a result, we likewise gain a firm northern border for the "right hand" tribal provinces, and a firm southern border for the "left hand" ones.

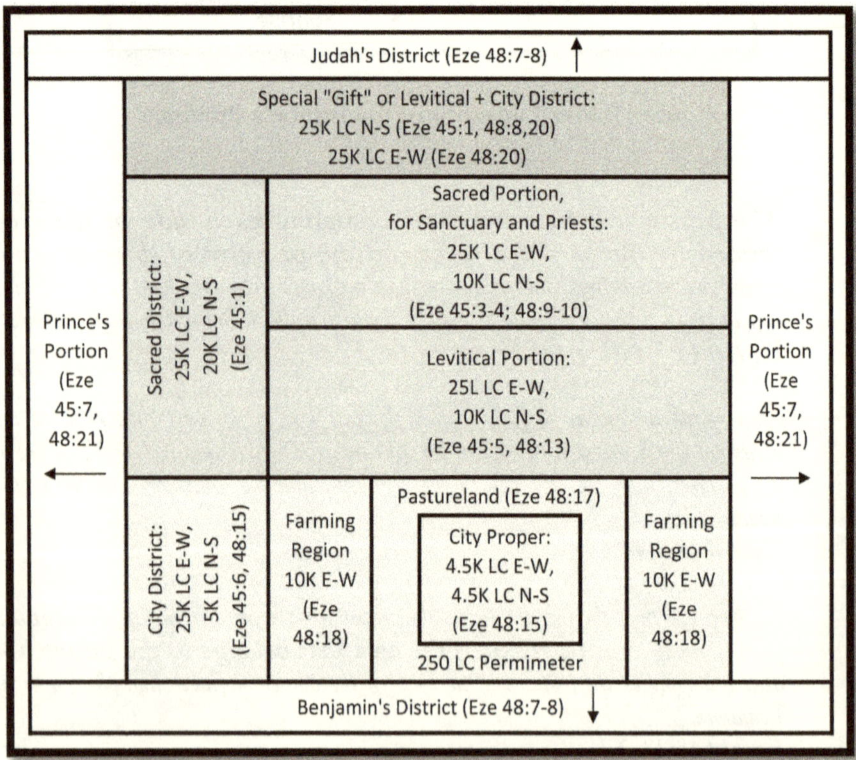

Figure 18: Sacred District Functional Diagram

The anchor point is, of course, Jerusalem. With Ezekiel 45:1-7, and amplification in 48:8-22, we are given detailed information on the sacred-plus-city[223] district, telling us how the City is situated within.

This information from Ezekiel can be further distilled into a map-like diagram:

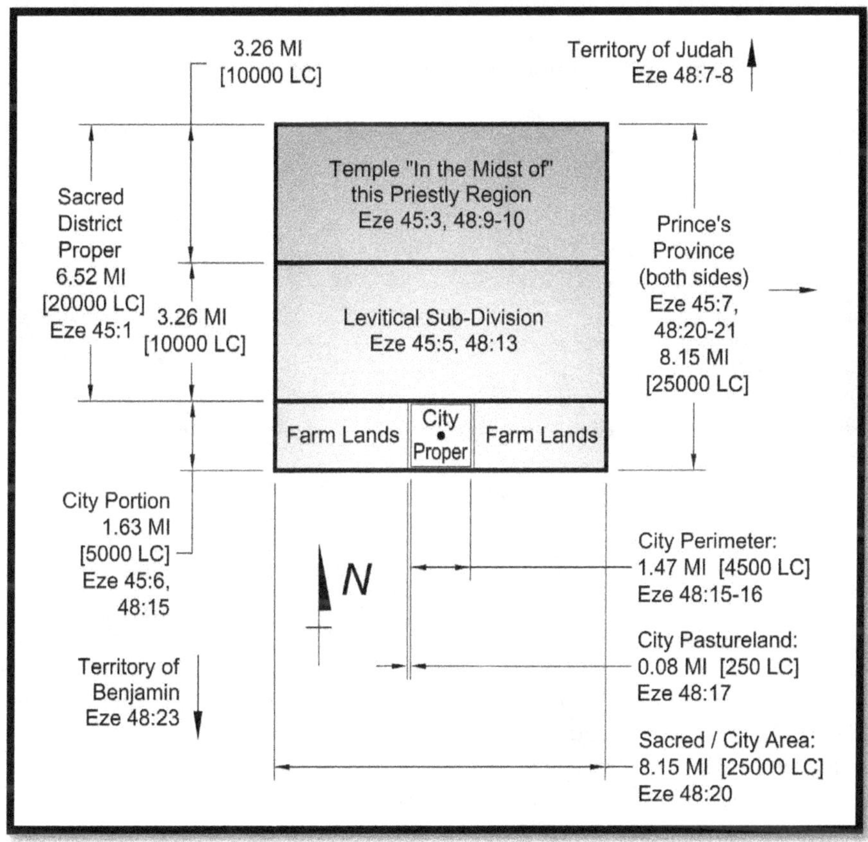

Figure 19: Sacred District Dimensional Diagram

[223] Technically, a scriptural distinction is made between the northern (20,000 long cubits, north to south) "Sacred District" (45:1 and 48:20) and the southern city section (5,000 long cubits, north to south) of land. In order to discuss these elements as a whole, and for the sake of brevity, I have elected to use the term "Sacred District" to describe the entire (25,000 cubit) square district that embraces both.

If one centers Jerusalem[224] within the box labeled "City Proper," one therefore has a good idea on where the northern and southern borders of the Prince's Province will lay.

A Mapping Summary

From what we have explored thus far, the Prince's Province can be overlaid on a (present-day) topographical map[225] as follows.

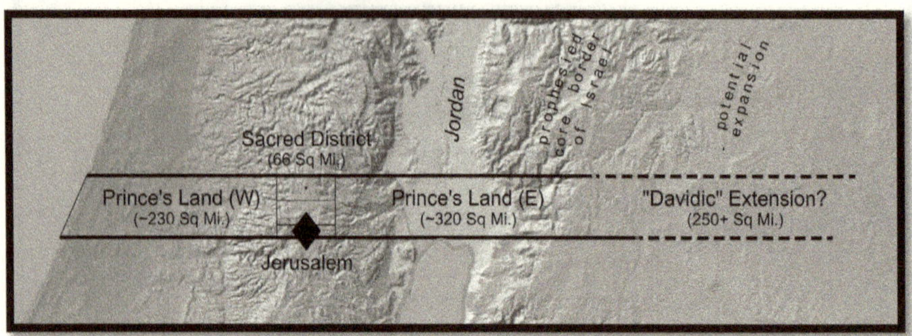

Figure 20: The Dedicated Region

This "cross section" of the land shows many of the geographic elements (discussed in Chapter 7) that most, or all, of the provinces share: coastal plains, main mountain range, the severe drop to the Jordan, and back up to the eastern highlands.

It also reminds us that we can't know exactly how far the eastward "Davidic" expansion will go, as discussed in Chapter 5. It practically *must* go as far as the line labeled "prophesied core border of Israel," which corresponds with the eastern border of the three eastern tribes (see Chapter 4). If that is the only expansion beyond Ezekiel's border, Jerusalem is actually centered (east-to-

[224] For "centering" purposes, whether ancient or contemporary Jerusalem is in view is beside the point for this particular journey. We are only roughly establishing certain key boundaries here.

[225] Topographic backgrounds here were obtained from Marine Geoscience Data Systems, and their online GMRT (Global Multi-Resolution Topography) Synthesis software, 6 January 2008, (http://www.marine-geo.org/tools/maps_grids.php). Ryan, W. B. F., S.M. Carbotte, J. Coplan, S. O'Hara, A. Melkonian, R. Arko, R.A. Weissel, V. Ferrini, A. Goodwillie, F. Nitsche, J. Bonczkowski, and R. Zemsky (2009), Global Multi-Resolution Topography (GMRT) synthesis data set, Geochem. Geophys. Geosyst., 10, Q03014, doi:10.1029/2008GC002332.

west) within the Prince's Province. But if David's holdings of Moab, Ammon and Edom are reacquired by the Son, His province will extend much further east, placing Jerusalem toward the western side. This is not an issue though, for the City is not required to be at the literal center[226] of the province.

Segmented Lands of the Prince

The Gifted Province

How does Messiah obtain ownership of the province? It is by way of a deliberate gift from the people.

> *Bordering the territory of Judah from east to west will be the portion* ***you are to present as a special gift.*** *It will be 25,000 cubits wide, and its length from east to west will equal one of the tribal portions; the sanctuary will be in the center of it. Ezekiel 48:8, NIV*

We are later told that the recipient of this gift will be the Prince – for He will own almost all of it[227]. Though the implied recipient in verse 8 above is God, it all makes sense because the Prince *is* God[228]. Thus God the Son will receive this dedicated gift of special land. Yet He will do so also as the Prince of Israel who dwells with His people: *Immanuel*, Son of David.

There will apparently be a major ceremony in which the tribes and their leaders stand before their Prince-King and Savior, and literally give Him title to this section of land. After He wins the Promised Land for them as the coming Joshua (Yeshua, Jesus), the people will be in a position to gift this land back to Him. What a wonderful cermony that will be!

A Reason for the Split

Something that jumps out from the topographical map above is how dramatically the Prince's land is clearly split into eastern and western sections.

[226] See Ezekiel 48:22 where the English word "center" is often translated. Note however that the word sometimes translated "central," *tavek* (Strong's OT:8432), does not necessarily mean exact center. That is, the Sacred District will not necessarily lay in the exact midpoint of the Prince's Province, but will be "in the midst" of it, enveloped by it.
[227] Ezekiel 48:21-22.
[228] E.g., Isaiah 9:6; John 1:1.

This wouldn't seem so odd, if it were not for the lack of connection between them, other than the Sacred District. Why would this be? That is, why would not the Prince's region be wider than the (25,000 LC-wide) Sacred district, and find connection all around it? Here are some candidate reasons.

- Perhaps the Prince wishes to make a clear statement, that His land and the Sacred District are one, even as the Father and He are one[229]. If the Prince's land surrounded the Sacred District, the two might seem segregated.

- Perhaps the Prince wishes to make His activities in His lands, Jerusalem and the Sacred District so intertwined that His passage between all is frequent and normal. "*The prince is to be among them, going in when they go in and going out when they go out*" (Ezekiel 46:10, NIV). For Him to get from His western lands to His eastern, there would be no getting around the Sacred District; nor would the Prince want there to be.

- Perhaps the Prince intends some important symbolism. For with this arrangement, His lands enfold, protect and honor both the Father's purposes within the Sacred District and Jerusalem His treasure, from sunrise to sunset, like wings of an eagle.

Most likely, all the above will be at work, along with further reasons and purposes the Lord alone knows. For the Lord is holding back many wonderful surprises[230].

The Gifted District

Let's next consider something that the Prince's *natural* father, David, did during his years as king. At his own expense King David secured and set aside a special area that would become the site of the most glorious Temple in prior history[231]. If one considers that his anointed Son will follow "in His father's footsteps," one could also surmise that Messiah will, after acquiring this special land, make a gift for the Father's purposes.

[229] E.g., John 10:30.
[230] Isaiah 64:4; 1 Corinthians 2:9.
[231] 2 Chronicles 3:1, in view of 2 Samuel 24:18-22 and 1 Chronicles 21:18-28.

Indeed, Ezekiel describes the Dedicated Region specifically as a gift[232] to God (the Father). The wording can be taken as a command by God to the Israelites to make this gift; but because the Prince represents Israel in this context[233], it is He giving the sacred gift of land. The wording can also be seen as God the Father commanding God the Son to make the gift; and He can, because the people have just given Him the title. Either way, the Prince does exactly what his natural father David did: He gives this most special section of *His* land, that embracing Jerusalem, to God the Father.

Indeed, we are told that the Sacred District contains "the best" of all the land[234]. Moreover, it contains the most holy areas that are to be used for the Temple[235]. In the spirit of his natural father, Yeshua will receive this land, and then grant the best of it to Father-God.

The Tithed Portion

There may be another special element to this gift by the Son to the Father, and it involves the idea of giving back the tithe of one's gains. As has been discussed, we don't know just how far Israel's borders might be extended to the east, and we must say the same for the Prince's province. We can but approximate the extremes at least. The Dedicated Region can be roughly calculated as follows:

---

232 Ezekiel 48:8, in which the sacred-plus-city district is explicitly described as a gift to God.

233 As king. For a deeper representation, see Isaiah 49 in which Messiah is clearly spoken of, and yet in verse 3 is named *Israel.*

234 Ezekiel 48:14.

235 Ezekiel 48:21

	Sq. Mi.	Sq. Km
Sacred District	66	106
Prince's Land (W)	229	369
Prince's Land (E)	319	513
Total Area (baseline)	**614**	**988**
Davidic Extension (max?)	250	402
Total Area (potential)	864	1390

Area of Sacred District as a Percentage of the Dedicated Region (Prince's Province)	
Per Ezekiel's "Baseline" Borders	11%
Per Extended / Potential Borders	8%
Average	10%

Figure 21: Areas of the Dedicated Region

What these approximations tell us is that the Sacred District will not only be quite large, they will be on the order of one-tenth the size of the Dedicated Region. Put differently, the Prince's deeded lands will be about ten times larger than those set aside for the entire Sacred District. We are reminded of this verse:

> *And all the tithe of the land, whether of the seed of the land, or of the fruit of the tree, is the Lord's: it is holy unto the Lord.*
> *Leviticus 27:30, KJV*

Not only will the Prince be giving a section of His property to the Lord, He may well specifically be granting a *tithe* of His land. Of course, all the Holy Land belongs to the God[236]; but this sacred gift portion is the Prince's honoring of that profound fact. In the end, if the Sacred District is an exact tithe, an eastern border position would be established. But we will draw the line at this point, and leave these mapping finalities to the Lord.

[236] E.g., Leviticus 25:23.

Chapter 7: Royal Welcoming

Nations will come to your light, and kings to the brightness of your dawn.

Isaiah 60:3, NIV

In that day the Root of Jesse will stand as a banner for the peoples; the nations will rally to him, and his place of rest will be glorious.

Isaiah 11:10, NIV

It is the glory of God to conceal a matter; to search out a matter is the glory of kings.

Proverbs 25:2, NIV

What the King's Lands Might Contain

From what has been observed, east and west of the Sacred District, the Prince will own somewhere between 550 and 850 square miles (352,000 to 544,000 acres; 1,425 to 2,200 square kilometers). That's a lot of land! What might Messiah do with such an expanse of property? What would Jesus do, if He held title to a massive, and most holy, section of the Promised Land? What activities might His lands accommodate?

Hints from Solomon

Though the Bible isn't explicit on this point, it does offer some hints – a prominent one being Solomon. Messiah was, is, and will remain, David's physical descendant and therefore "son." Now to Solomon. Though that ancient king succumbed to idolatry in his later years[237], he was nevertheless the direct offspring of David, and (in earlier years) prophetically illustrative of the coming king of kings. In his 'glory days,' Solomon embodied the fact that God would someday send the ultimate King. But this One will never fall, will never die, and will always surpass all that David's directly-born son accomplished. Lord Yeshua claimed that He was far greater than His foretelling older brother[238]. Thus He remains the fulfillment and answer to Solomon's foreshadow.

Messiah will come in the heart and strength of David, and the wisdom and glory of Solomon. Jesus will not dismiss the hopes and achievements of David and Solomon, but – if anything – *complete* them, in fullness of brilliance and meaningfulness.

When we understand the prophetic nature of Solomon's accomplishments (in his earlier days of obedience), and his prophetic position as the foreshadowing "Son of David," new facets emerge to discussion of the final Son of David, and what He might accomplish. As to what the Prince will decide to do with His lands, we can therefore learn a lot from what Solomon, and his father David of course, did under similar presaging circumstances.

---

237 1 Kings 11.

238 Matthew 12:42; Luke 11:31.

Hints from Surrounding Activities

The Bible also refers to many things happening in the Promised Land on the horizon, many of which involve the Prince and resources at His disposal. So if we see that the Prince has certain responsibilities, or that He will tend to provide for certain needs, we can also see that space will be required to satisfy them. Sometimes a lot of space. Though we need to caveat all with "it's up to Him," the Lord does not discourage us from connecting the dots.

Enabling Enterprises

Provision for Horses

We'll begin the land-usage candidates with one that is fun, and easy to lay down evidence for: Where will the King put all His horses?

Solomon, as you may well know, was a very great fan of horses. Some of his interest was by way of animal physiology[239]. Unfortunately though, his main interest in the horse was in its utility in warfare, so much so that he built many cities dedicated to his fleets of horses and chariots[240]. Solomon accumulated these horses (and therefore these facilities) in direct defiance of Moses' law[241]. And with the division and declination of his kingdom during the reign of his sons, all that horsepower evaporated into history, having gained nothing.

Even so, the fact of all those horses remains a historical fact of Solomon's aura, in the height of his glory. The question is, will David's ultimate Son, Messiah, provide analogous facilities for His own horses? Do Solomon's vast equine holdings bear any precedent for Yeshua's activities, and thus His lands?

These may seem strange questions to put forward. However, they strongly relate to a factual and very horse-related issue in the Prince's time. For indeed, many thousands of *His* war horses *will* be present. Now, the horses I am referring to are *not* the many ones harnessed for battle on the side of the Lord's enemies, in the huge and conclusive battle that is often called Armageddon[242].

---

[239] 1 Kings 4:33.

[240] 1 Kings 10:26; 2 Chronicles 1:14, 8:6.

[241] Deuteronomy 17:16b. Worse, he did so by way of Egypt (1 Kings 10:28), in a trade relationship explicitly forbidden – especially in regards to horses (Deuteronomy 17:16b).

[242] Though the Bible abounds with references to this conclusive battle of the current age, this term (see Revelation 16:16 for its only Scriptural instance) has generally become the name for that battle.

The simple fact is that those particular horses will suffer the same fate as their riders[243]. Rather, I am referring to an immense number of war horses also involved with that earthly battle, though on the other side:

> *The* ***armies of heaven*** *were following him,* ***riding on white horses*** *and dressed in fine linen, white and clean.*
> *Revelation 19:14, NIV*

These horses, all of them white, will come from Heaven. They will be just as real as the riders upon them; and the effect of both, upon the losers of Armageddon, will be as physical and deadly as one could imagine.

Where do those riders go, after this great battle? They remain on Earth as subjects of Messiah's coming dominion[244]. That fact is a very big hint toward what happens to their horses: in all likelihood, they will remain on Earth as well. If that is the case, there will be a whole lot of big, white, strong war horses of Heavenly origin, many present within Israel, just after Messiah has completed His great victory. Since warfare will no longer be a phenomenon, these horses will need something else to do. They will need a place to go, and a new purpose in life on this earth.

The quantities of these horses will not be insignificant. If the number of their riders from Heaven is beyond personal calculation[245], somewhere north of the (calculable) number of 100,000,000[246], we are speaking of a lot of horses. Perhaps many will stay with their riders, wherever they go, to distant homelands or near. Be that as it may, the Prince has ultimate responsibility of the horses, and many may end up under His direct care[247].

So, the initial question bears re-asking: Where will the King put all His horses? We have, actually, an answer based on precedent. In view of Solomon's horse-cities, in view of his and Messiah's[248] love for horses, and in view of the presence of this great quantity of horses that have fought in His service[249], there seems an easy solution. That is, the Prince will, like his "brother" Solomon, order the building of great stables for these marvelous creatures, along with

---

243 Zechariah 14:12-15, particularly the last verse.

244 See Revelation 19-20, while keeping in view the criticality of "fine linen" and whiteness of robes (and horses, for that matter) for these saints of all nations.

245 Revelation 7:9.

246 10,000 squared, a reckonable number: Revelation 5:11.

247 For example, certain gentile believers then will be chosen by God to serve Him in the Temple (Isaiah 56:6-8), and their "heavenly horses" may revert to the Prince who created them.

248 Especially seen in the Creator's personal love for horses, in Job 39.

249 See Job 39:18-25, for a depiction of how greatly God feels about His creation in this animal, particularly when it is unleashed in a battle context.

infrastructure for not only their care, but for people who desire to visit them and ride upon them again. All of that takes acreage, and a lot of it.

Provision for Offerings

Sacrifices are much involved in the Millennial period, with purposes toward memorial, rather than atonement. We will not get into these weighty theological matters here, except to point out that the Prince will have a major role in providing for these offerings:

> *It will be the duty of the prince to provide the burnt offerings, grain offerings and drink offerings at the festivals, the New Moons and the Sabbaths — at all the appointed feasts of the house of Israel. He will provide the sin offerings, grain offerings, burnt offerings and fellowship offerings to make atonement for the house of Israel.*
> *Ezekiel 45:17, NIV*

Without question, a lot of animals are potentially involved for these purposes, which means a lot of grazing land and stables for the animals. It also means lands for vineyards (drink offerings) and fields (grain offerings).

Does all this agriculture need to happen within the Prince's land? No, for the Prince's provision may refer to His payment for products raised and harvested in other tribal provinces. For example, we are pointedly informed that the coastlands in general will be places of sheep raising[250]. Even so, the good possibility remains that at least some of His lands may be assigned for purposes of raising livestock and crops, on a perhaps not insignificant scale.

Provision for Shipping

Prince's land has as its western border the Mediterranean Sea. And though the present coastline may not be exactly the same in Messiah's day[251], it will remain a coastline, with all the features a coastline permits. This fact invites other ideas of land use up and down the entire coast – including the coastline belonging to the Prince.

Solomon had an enormous fleet of ships, bringing gold and other forms of wealth to the capitol of his day, Zion[252]. Many references indicate similar and

---

[250] See Zephaniah 2:6-7.

[251] In view of the extensive terra-forming alluded to in so many prophecies, throughout the Bible, related to the "Day of the Lord."

[252] 1 Kings 9:26-28; 2 Chronicles 8:17-18, 9:21.

great wealth being brought to Jerusalem in Messiah's time[253]. Solomon did not have his own province; but the Prince will. It would not be surprising then if areas on the Prince's coast were related to purposes of shipping.

On this western edge of the Prince's land, this maritime aspect almost goes without saying. Zebulun, as we have seen, will be known for its ports; and since ships need a place to go to, and come from, we can expect other ports all along the coast: for inter-tribal shipping will be arguably plentiful. Given the wealth being specifically transported to Jerusalem, the Prince's ports will most likely be major ones, and busy. Ports involve docks, maintenance facilities, roads, lots or workers, and surrounding towns to support them. All of this takes up a large amount of property.

Further, vast staging grounds will be needed. In providing for the construction of "Solomon's" Temple, King David amassed construction materials[254] on a scale requiring some serious real estate. With the truly massive structures foreseen by Ezekiel for the Temple, the coming Son of David will likewise provide areas for staging of materials until they are immediately required on the construction site. This means huge warehouses or lay-down areas. With the enormous gates and walls prophesied by Ezekiel, the real estate requirements for material storage, at least in the early years of Messiah's rule, will not be small.

Provision for Highways

We have seen that the Prince's province will transect the nation of Israel, leaving no way to travel between northern and southern provinces except through His land[255]. This seems deliberate: for in the normal and day-to-day needs of transportation between the northern tribes and the southern, the Prince is set in the midst of his "brothers," His lands between those finally assigned to the sons and tribes of Jacob-Israel. Though the Southern and Northern Kingdoms of Israel were divided in ancient times, just *after* Solomon, in Messiah's day they will be made as one:

> *I will make them one nation in the land, on the mountains of Israel. There will be one king over all of them and they will never again be two nations or be divided into two kingdoms.*
> *Ezekiel 37:22, NIV*

---

[253] E.g., Isaiah 60.
[254] I Chronicles 22.
[255] Additional provision for north-south communication will surely be by means of the Sacred District, as is indicated in Isaiah 19:23-25.

Clearly, the Prince will not allow His own land to present an obstacle between north and south, but will instead greatly facilitate the physical communication between the two.

As an example of commercial north-south transportation needs, Scripture explicitly says that certain regions of Millennial Israel will specialize in the production of one thing, while other regions in another[256]. Throughout this bustle of agricultural[257] and other forms of trade between the tribal provinces, the Prince's province will not be a barrier. North-to-south highways will most likely proceed through His lands at various points. One major such highway will indeed exist through the Sacred District[258]. But for less sacred purposes of transport, for movement of the vast amount of people and goods between the northern tribal provinces and the southern, several other north-south highways through the Prince's Province can be anticipated.

These routes will not be simple paths. For as we will see later, those traversing the western land of the Prince must traverse one major river; and those crossing His eastern land, but west of the Jordan valley, must span two. Since it will be a garden-like region in high demand with travelers, we can expect facilities for those that wish to stop and see the rivers, gaze at the Prince's wonderful gardens, explore the history and walls of ancient cities resurrected, and on and on. All of these north-to-south passages therefore involve paved and drained highways, with significant bridges, retaining walls, overviews, and other engineered structures.

The Prince will facilitate such needs foreseen in Scripture and anticipated by the prophecies. In doing so, we can expect Him to employ His architects, engineers, construction workers and landscape artists to bring about those facilities. The many wonderful highways, byways, ports, staging areas, major bridges, small bridges, footpaths, viewing plazas and shelters will be the result of His master design and clear direction. And of course, He will provide the real estate for all this to happen, both in the construction phase and permanently, as He deems required. We can remind ourselves of what Solomon said: "*I undertook great projects…*" (Ecclesiastes 2:4a, NIV).

[256] E.g., as we have seen, lumber production from Lebanon (here basically absorbed by certain northern tribes), per Isaiah 60:13; sheep raising, in ancient coastal areas of the Philistines, per Zephaniah 2:6-7; fish, in the Dead Sea (Benjamin & Simeon) area, per Ezekiel 47:8-10; and so on.

[257] E.g., Leviticus 26:3-12; Deuteronomy 30:3-9.

[258] Addressed in the beginning of Chapter 7.

Residential Regions

Accommodations for Workers

Without question, the above "enterprises" taking place in the Prince's lands are only examples. There will surely be other occupations involved, such as those related to gardening, food services, artwork, music, and a host of other things.

All these activities require workers, and workers need homes for themselves and their families. True, the Province is only 8.15 miles (13.1 kilometers) wide, and workers could easily ride horses, wagons, or other vehicles for the commute. Or, having the sort of healthy bodies that Isaiah prophesied[259], they could walk or even run to work. There is every reason, however, for the Prince to make accommodation for His faithful workers and "servants," and not push them into Judah or Benjamin for their abodes. These are people that wish to be near the Prince and work directly for Him[260]; and we can anticipate that He will truly be a wonderful host.

Accommodations for Guests (Part 1)

Other than these many workers and their families, will the prince live alone in His lands? No, for He will surely have many guests. We can take Solomon for an example, with him having hosted many foreign dignitaries, and hosted them well. The story of the Queen of Sheba comes to mind, as does all the lavish accoutrements and services she witnessed[261]. The Prince will likewise be visited by many kings, of all nations. There are many other Scriptures that bear on this point[262], with these as just some examples:

> *Abraham will surely become a great and powerful nation, and all nations on earth will be blessed through him.*
> *Genesis 18:18, NIV*

---

259 E.g., Isaiah 65:20.
260 E.g., Isaiah 60:9-10.
261 1 Kings 10; 2 Chronicles 9.
262 See also, for example, Psalms 68:29, 72:11, 102:15-16; Isaiah 49:7, 49:23, 62:2; Revelation 15:4, 17:14, 21:24.

The nobles of the nations assemble as the people of the God of Abraham, for the kings of the earth belong to God; he is greatly exalted.
Psalms 47:9, NIV

May all the kings of the earth praise you, O LORD, when they hear the words of your mouth. 5 May they sing of the ways of the LORD, for the glory of the LORD is great.
Psalms 138:4-5, NIV

In the last days the mountain of the LORD's temple will be established as chief among the mountains; it will be raised above the hills, and all nations will stream to it.
Isaiah 2:2, NIV

Nations will come to your light, and kings to the brightness of your dawn.
Isaiah 60:3, NIV

Your gates will always stand open, they will never be shut, day or night, so that men may bring you the wealth of the nations — their kings led in triumphal procession.
Isaiah 60:11, NIV

At that time they will call Jerusalem The Throne of the LORD, and all nations will gather in Jerusalem to honor the name of the LORD.
Jeremiah 3:17a, NIV

On his robe and on his thigh he has this name written: KING OF KINGS AND LORD OF LORDS.
Revelation 19:16, NIV

Without question, the focus of all this kingly and international attention will be upon the Sacred District, for it will contain both the Lord's holy City and the great Temple of the Name of God the Father. At the same time, Messiah bears the holy Name[263], and remains the physical expression of the Father[264]. There is no doubt then that the kings of the Earth will seek out personal interaction with the Prince, in an in-depth manner.

In that day the Root of Jesse will stand as a banner for the peoples; ***the nations will rally to him, and his place of rest will be glorious.***
Isaiah 11:10, NIV

263 Exodus 23:20-22.

264 E.g., Colossians 1:19-20, 2:9-10.

Where is this "place of rest" for the Son of David? Exactly where we are "standing" in our journey: within His lands, His inheritance[265]. We can take Isaiah's word for it that this resting place will be glorious, including all the activities within it. As a witness of all this, we have a profound precursor, not from a king, but a queen: the Queen of Sheba. Her effusive descriptions of Solomon's court resound to this day, and serve as a foreshadowing voice in that coming chorus of world rulers that will bow to the great Prince, and thrill to His Person and hospitality.

Where will all these kings and queens reside, when they come to visit Jerusalem? Who will put up the international crowds that "rally to Him" on an ongoing basis? Surely, the City proper will be packed with permanent inhabitants[266] and other features, and may therefore lack the room. But the Prince, the ultimate host, will ensure that kings and queens, their (sometimes enormous) retinues, and all other visitors, will be more than adequately accommodated.

Accommodations for Guests (Part 2)

Another way to consider the Prince's guests is from the more intimate perspective of "wife" who dwells with Him. Messiah's "wife" is His people, God's gathered people as a whole[267], an *Israel* expanded in a covenant that reaches out to *all* nations[268]. The final expression of this eternal wedding will come after the Millennial period[269]:

> *I saw the* ***Holy City****, the new* ***Jerusalem****, coming down out of heaven from God,* ***prepared as a bride*** *beautifully dressed for her husband...* ***"Come, I will show you the bride, the wife of the Lamb."***
> *Revelation 21:2, 9b, NIV*

But before then, during the Prince's thousand-year reign on earth, will there be symbols of Him dwelling with His "Bride"? Yes: the City of Jerusalem itself, enfolded by the eastern and western wings of the Prince's land.

---

265 Though it can be said that Jesus rested in Heaven after his suffering for our atonement, the context of the above verse is clearly during His reign as king, wherein this creation finds peace and this world obtains healing.

266 Psalms 122:1-4.

267 E.g., Psalms 45:9; Isaiah 49:18, 61:10, 62:5; Ephesians 5:31-32.

268 As foreseen in the Lord's unbreakable blessing on Abraham, and confirmed in, e.g., Ephesians 2:11-13, 3:6.

269 Revelation 20.

Is there another outworking of the "wife's accommodations" in the Prince's lands? Perhaps Solomon gives us another hint. Pharaoh's daughter was that king's first wife; and though he cheated on her by accumulating numerous other wives[270], there is the profound monument that Solomon made for her alone: a dedicated palace on a par with his own[271]. Now, Egypt was the initial human venue from which the nation of Israel was redeemed[272], and is also figurative of the world at large from whence the Lord will extract for Himself an eternal bride[273]. When combined with the idea of all nations comprising the "bride" of the Prince, Solomon's first wife may well be symbolic: The Egyptian bride, for whom a lavish palace was specially built. If so, this would simply speak to the glorious accommodations for international visitors to Messiah's lands. They are just as much a part of His "beloved," His "Bride"; and the Prince will readily welcome these guests.

Accommodations for Relatives

In addition to workers and guests of the Prince, there is one more reason for residential land use in His province, seen in this whopper of a puzzle:

> *This is what the Sovereign LORD says: If* **the prince** *makes a gift from* **his inheritance** *to one of* **his sons**, *it will also belong to* **his descendants;** *it is to be their property by inheritance. 17 If, however, he makes a gift from his inheritance to one of his servants, the servant may keep it until the year of freedom; then it will revert to the prince. His inheritance belongs to* **his sons** *only; it is theirs. 18 The prince must not take any of the inheritance of the people, driving them off their property. He is to give* **his sons** *their inheritance out of his own property, so that none of my people will be separated from his property.*
> *Ezekiel 46:16-18, NIV*

Does this mean the Prince will get married and have children? No, it is only saying *if*. The focus is not on the Prince's offspring, but on the fact that nothing will take away from the lands of Israelites under His rule – not even the Prince, in granting any inheritance to His sons (*if* He had any).

---

[270] In direct defiance of Mosaic law (Deuteronomy 17:17), Solomon's harems are almost as legendary as his wisdom.
[271] 1 Kings 7:8.
[272] Egypt was the initial human venue from which the nation of Israel was redeemed, as seen in the Pentateuch, the Psalms and the Prophets; see also the plagues of Revelation, in light of the plagues upon Egypt in the original Passover.
[273] E.g., Hosea 8:13; Revelation 11:8.

But why would Ezekiel put this reassurance to Israel in this fashion? Perhaps several reasons – beginning with the reassurance to the prophet's original audience that the ultimate Prince will not steal any lands from the public, even if He has the power to do so. But there is further reassurance, of a different sort. This basic idea of having sons is an obvious requirement: for a royal prince is one in a chain, father to son. Under normal circumstances, to break that chain would be a sign of weakness in the royalty, and eventual doom for the nation[274]. Ezekiel is also indicating that royal progeniture will not die out[275].

But these are not normal circumstances on the horizon: for the coming Prince, the King of kings, is immortal already, and will be forever[276]. His kingdom – ruled by *Him*, and no other – will have no end:

> *Of the increase of his government and peace there will be no end. He will reign on David's throne and over his kingdom, establishing and upholding it with justice and righteousness from that time on and forever. The zeal of the LORD Almighty will accomplish this.*
> *Isaiah 9:7, NIV*

This subject of whether or not Messiah would have children is brought up by Isaiah, but in the negative. In Messiah's first coming to bear the sins and wounds of mankind, He would be prematurely slain, and thus denied physical offspring[277]. If that were the end of the story, it would be truly devastating to all the Biblical promises. But it was not: Messiah arose from the grave! All that waits is for Him to receive David's throne, in the Father's timing.

The need for Messiah to have sons, for the purposes of royal progeny, is therefore a moot point: for He will never again die. On the other hand, will the Prince-King have sons and daughters of His own? Actually, yes! For any child of God is made so through the sacrifice the Prince has already made. This is why we can refer to Jesus-Yeshua not only as *Prince*, but also as *Father.*

---

[274] Ezekiel's prophecies here, as do many others of the First Testament, provide fully for "plan A," that is, Israel's having accepted Messiah in His coming as the lamb-redeemer, a la Isaiah 53. The outcomes of that potentiality, including the idea of the Prince's having a human wife and literal sons, and the loss of opportunity for any other nation to come into covenant with the Lord (see, e.g., Deuteronomy 32:21; Romans 10-11) were always provided for in the prophecies. Such potentialities, however, are merely hypothetical at this point. Israel *did* reject, and all nations *were* welcomed in. Even so, Israel's original promises remain in effect.

[275] Promised in, e.g., Psalms 89:35-36.

[276] E.g., Psalms 145:13; Micah 5:2; Luke 1:32-33; Hebrews 5:6, 7:3.

[277] Isaiah 53:8.

For to us a child is born… And he will be called… Everlasting ***Father, Prince*** *of Peace.*
Isaiah 9:6, NIV, excerpts

This makes any "child of the Prince" a candidate for what Ezekiel was talking about: that they will *not* receive inheritance-gifts of land in other (tribal) provinces on the basis of being a child of the Prince. All believers will be. So if believer-children want to live in those other provinces, we have already seen that they are welcome to do so. But land-transfers of this sort because of biological progeniture will not be known.

So, what *does* Ezekiel's puzzling passage say about an immortal Prince, with the entire population of His country (and beyond) as His "children"? First, if Prince wishes, He can make special gifts of *His* land to certain sons and daughters. Presumably, these recipients must agree to live there – as opposed to another tribal province, or their own regions of national ancestry. They (and *their* offspring) will own this property, in perpetuity.

Second, the Prince may well do the same for special servants, perhaps those closely involved with one of the many activities taking place in His lands or in the Sacred District. If the land granting is made on that basis, the properties are deeded over for only fifty-year increments of duration[278]. There is no requirement that these people (and their offspring) live there for more than that period of time. Given the longevity in this day, however, fifty years may seem quite brief[279].

Either way, these are additional residential properties within the land of the Prince. Some will be used for permanent residence, others for special servants dwelling there on a fifty-year rotational basis. In either case, these residents will be spiritual sons (and daughters) of our Lord and Prince; and they will add their voices to the ongoing choruses of praise to Him, their beloved Master, Savior and King.

---

278 The "year of freedom" being the Year of Jubilee: Leviticus 25:11.

279 Isaiah 65:20; Revelation 20:6.

Accommodations for the Prince

The Prince's main palace will be a place of formal communication and legislation, located in Jerusalem:

> *And many people shall go and say, Come ye, and let us go up to the mountain of the Lord, to the house of the God of Jacob; and he will teach us of his ways, and we will walk in his paths:* ***for out of Zion shall go forth the law, and the word of the Lord from Jerusalem.*** *4 And he shall judge among the nations, and shall rebuke many people…*
> *Isaiah 2:3-4a, KJV*

If Solomon's "House of the Forest of Lebanon"[280] is any indicator, this particular "place of rest" for Messiah will be glorious indeed[281]. But what of His own lands? Will the Prince have a home in His own property, apart from the main palace in Jerusalem? In view of all the other activities that may happen within His lands, it would not be surprising if He did dwell there. Further, since the Prince's Province is so similar to all the others in arrangement and size, it would be surprising if He did *not* live in it and literally dwell therein, amongst the tribes, alongside His brothers.

What form this residence might take, what scale, and whether the Prince will have one in both His east and west regions, we cannot say. But to that point, perhaps another statement of Solomon's has bearing:

> *I undertook great projects:* ***I built houses for myself*** *and planted vineyards.*
> *Ecclesiastes 2:4, NIV*

Such residence(s) will occupy real estate. Indeed, this royal home (or homes) within His province may well become the hub(s) of all activity and communication within the Prince's lands.

---

280 1 Kings 7:1-12.

281 Isaiah 11:10.

Fellowship Facilities

In addition to industrial and residential land usage, there is one more way the Prince may choose to employ His lands: for *civil* purposes. Though no explicit prophecies describe one public institution or another in His lands, we can examine what Solomon did, see what the coming circumstances are, and perhaps connect a few more dots.

Facilitation of Guidance

Solomon's wisdom was not merely legendary: for God's word explicitly informs us that no other king of the Earth was as gifted in this regard as he[282]. Solomon's wisdom, however, was not some prodigious natural talent he was born with. Rather, it was a supernatural gift bestowed on him by God[283] at about the time of his inauguration as David's successor[284]. It was because of such divinely-sourced wisdom that rulers of other countries came to hear him, and were astounded as a result – the main example offered being the Queen of Sheba.

In Messiah, we can expect similar dynamics. He, the "root of Jesse" and culminating successor to David, will likewise have this special form of wisdom[285] that can only come from the mind and heart of God Himself. This is because Jesus *is* God, and *one with* the Father[286]. Thus the divine wisdom will once again invite all those that hear of it, and instruct them – even the highest authorities of that day – in a profound and astounding manner. In that day, in the new political economy that only the Lord will have been able to create, the world's rulers will seek out the big answers for their constituencies. As Solomon said,

> *It is the glory of God to conceal a matter; to search out a matter is the glory of kings.*
> *Proverbs 25:2, NIV*

---

[282] E.g., 1 Kings 10:4-8, 23-24; 2 Chronicles 9:3-7, 22-23.

[283] As for the supernatural nature of Solomon's wisdom, see 1 Kings 4:29-34, 5:12; 2 Chronicles 1:10-12.

[284] 1 Kings 3:9-13; cf. 4:29-34, 5:12.

[285] E.g., Isaiah 11:1-2; also evident in 9:6-7.

[286] John 10:30.

To search out a matter, and find its resolution, will indeed be the glory of kings at that time. They will seek and find *definitive* knowledge in the *absolute* wisdom of the Creator, *in person*; and they will bask in the glory of the divine guidance.

Will there be facilities for such meetings between King Yeshua and kings of the world? Yes, without a doubt; and most likely, in a palace, and in Jerusalem. But these potentates will have travelled great distances, so it is likely that the Prince will receive them as guests in His own land, as discussed earlier. And if so, nearby places of more intimate meeting and counsel would also seem anticipated.

Facilitation of Learning

Additional aspects of Biblically-described wisdom include practical and technical knowledge, and the ability to teach at that level as well. With Solomon, this was precisely the case:

> *God gave Solomon wisdom and very great insight, and a breadth of understanding as measureless as the sand on the seashore. 30 Solomon's wisdom was greater than the wisdom of all the men of the East, and greater than all the wisdom of Egypt. 31 He was wiser than any other man... And his fame spread to all the surrounding nations... 33* ***He described plant life, from the cedar of Lebanon to the hyssop that grows out of walls. He also taught about animals and birds, reptiles and fish.*** *34 Men of all nations came to listen to Solomon's wisdom, sent by all the kings of the world, who had heard of his wisdom.*
> *1 Kings 4:29-31a, 31c, 33-34* NIV

Aided by divine gifting, Solomon taught on all manner of subjects from international politics down to detailed aspects of botany and biology. Having the very knowledge of God, our Creator and coming King will easily teach and minister in a similar manner, indeed far more so[287].

In Messiah's being a teacher to people of all nations, what might the implications be for how He might use His land? Surely, we can expect that large audiences will be involved. One can easily envision formal teaching facilities accommodating vast numbers of students, perhaps involving one or more amphitheaters or other such structures.

We also can expect that, like His forbear Solomon, King Yeshua will teach on subjects covering the entire spectrum of knowledge. As a case in point, Millennial environmental conditions will require a huge dissemination of new

[287] Seen in the fact of Solomon's being a foreshadowing of Messiah, and in that Yeshua was (Matthew 12:42, Luke 11:31), is, and will be greater than he. Also seen in Jesus having been frequently referred to as "teacher."

information, and across the whole population of Earth of that time. For due to *changes* in the biology of both animals[288] and plants[289] (a subject on which Solomon was supreme specialist), there will be many things that need to be taught in regards to agriculture. If only a certain percentage of national representatives were to be directly taught by the Prince, we are still talking about facilities permitting very large audiences.

As for other subjects for mankind to receive instruction on, we could cite new political boundaries, new civic regulations, and the unleashing of physical and engineering secrets known only to the Creator Himself[290].

Beyond auditoriums or amphitheaters, will there be classroom settings, or colleges? Again, we are not told. But since the Prince is the apex of all knowledge and its dissemination, we can understand that He would especially inform groups of teachers, who would then inform others[291]. If so, will such "colleges" only reside in the far-flung national territories, close to homes of students? Or will at least some be located in the Prince's lands? Time will tell.

While we don't know the particulars, we do know the Prince will accommodate, to at least some degree, teaching purposes such as those described. If He chooses to construct in His lands huge theaters, schools and other facilities toward those ends, we should not be too surprised. Moreover, they would be but one example of the Prince's own "great projects," for which Solomon's may serve as foreshadow and analog[292].

---

[288] E.g., the herbivorous and tame trend of wildlife in general per Isaiah 11:6-9, in the new covenant the Lord will make with nature in that time to come (e.g., Ezekiel 34:25; Hosea 2:18; Romans 8:19-21).

[289] In the huge number of Scriptures that speak to botanic renewal, a general subject addressed as we go along in these discussions.

[290] To agree that Yeshua-Jesus is the Creator (John 1:1-14; Colossians 1:16; Hebrews 1:1-2, 2:10) is also to agree that His utter knowledge of the mechanics of nature is unbounded and exhaustive, and that any ultimate solutions and potential inventions related to, say, physics, energy, and natural cooperation, are known to Him. For the Millennial period, there may therefore be an engineering revolution far beyond anything the world has known, yet at the same time being one that is harmonious with the restored (and "Edenic") environment. Such matters, in all their detail, are huge candidates for the Prince's teaching, so that needs of both humankind and all creation are cooperatively and simultaneously satisfied. The same kind of argument applies to all other branches of knowledge and nature, e.g., science, design, art, and engineering.

[291] Perhaps in some reflection of Moses' organization of the judges (Exodus 18:22-26).

[292] Ecclesiastes 2:4.

Facilitation of the Arts

Though many other forms of civic facilities may be built by the Prince in His lands, we will take just this one further candidate here: facilities for the arts.

King David, the maternal "father" of Messiah, was very much into the arts. For an example of his personal talents, in a great expression of joy over the permanent dwelling place for the Lord's Name, David danced in an extravagant fashion[293]. David consistently expressed his love for God in music (with the harp, probably also signing), and also through poetry (in his psalms). He could also draw: for David drew up the plans for the Temple, as the Lord God inspired him[294]. As for the tactile arts, David amassed gold, silver, gems, and other articles of value and beauty so that the Temple would be glorious[295].

By many avenues then, the artistic heart of David had its manifestations. With Messiah, the ultimate Son of David, one would expect no less an emphasis. Yeshua is, after all, *the* Creator[296]. In regards to how the Prince will utilize His lands then, the arts may well be prominently represented and facilitated. In view of the artistic passions of David and the masterworks of Solomon (the Temple, two palaces, and other major public works), there will surely be analogies with the coming Son of David.

For example, and quite in line with expressions of David, there may well be public performances of many forms in the Messianic era, focusing on dance, music, poetry, or other of the performance arts. Such performances invite a theater of some sort. And since the audiences will be potentially gigantic, we might expect such facilities to be correspondingly massive. Whether enclosed theaters or exposed amphitheaters, the seating areas may be vast. And from the perspective of variety in artistic expression, there may well be more than one such facility – perhaps numerous ones.

I've mentioned mainly the performance arts; but what of the others, such as visual (e.g., painting), plastic (sculpture and architecture), and textile? Since we know that such artistic results will be profoundly present in the Temple to come[297], the Prince may well personally enable and encourage these activities, across most (if not all) such artistic forms. If He does, surely such expressions

---

[293] 2 Samuel 6:14-15.

[294] 1 Chronicles 28:2,11-12.

[295] E.g., 2 Samuel 8:7, with the eventual metallurgic result with Solomon seen in 1 Kings 10:16-17.

[296] John 1:3, 10; Ephesians 3:9; Colossians 1:16; Hebrews 1:2.

[297] With the precedent of the Tabernacle (whose art is well described in Exodus), and also Solomon's Temple.

will be multi-national in origin. And, based on the following facts and references, it will not be a small artistic "expression."

- Full worship of the Lord involves all one's being[298]
- Many artists, of *all* cultures, will be involved[299]
- These artist will be fully freed to worship the Lord[300]
- They will do so, starting in their own lands[301]
- But, they will also bring their glory to Jerusalem[302]

From these points, we can expect there to be a huge and continual flood of art objects, of all compositions, directed toward the epicenter of the world's worship in praise of God Almighty. And that's a lot of art.

Will the Prince choose to display these tangible expressions of praise to God, for those that wish to see them and echo their message? Will He enable such displays with (perhaps quite large) exhibition facilities, such as galleries or museums, in His own land? Perhaps with Solomon, we see hints: in the numerous crafted musical instruments he had made[303], in the sculpted lions that adorned the steps to his throne[304], and in his displaying of the 200 golden shields in the House of the Forest of Lebanon[305].

What we can know for sure is that Prince Yeshua is the supreme artist, for He was, and remains, *The Creator.* One way or another, it is fully understandable that He will amply provide for the creative expressions of all His people, especially in their worship of God the Father, for it is but His creative and Holy Spirit they will be responding to.

Summary of the Garden

Though the Prince's lands will be large, we have seen many reasons for them to be. Many people, from around the world, will come to enjoy His teaching, and the array of art that will flourish under His care. Residences will also be present for those that come to dwell with the Prince, some permanently,

---

298 Deuteronomy 6:5; Mark 12:30; Luke 10:27.

299 E.g., Zechariah 2:11, 8:22; Revelation 7:9.

300 In the absence of Satan's influence (Revelation 20:1-7).

301 *The nations on every shore will worship him, every one in its own land* (Zephaniah 2:11b, NIV).

302 Psalms 86:9; reflective of the same eternal phenomenon, per Revelation 21:26.

303 1 Kings 10:12.

304 1 Kings 10:19-20.

305 1 Kings 10:16-17.

some for a number of years, others for only a brief period. Various enterprises will supply these and many other needs of the day, particularly those of the holy Temple. And facilitating all will be major highways, lesser roads, and other infrastructure.

Without question, there will be a lot going on in this long, 8.15-mile-wide, focal strip of Israel's land on the horizon. And on top of all the candidate land uses, this "Dedicated Region" will also be a special garden in its own right. And that is the subject of our final leg of this journey.

Chapter 8: Eden Arising

I have come into my garden, my sister, my bride…

Song of Solomon 5:1a, NIV

…Adam, who was a pattern of the one to come.

Romans 5:14b, NIV

For, behold, I create new heavens and a new earth: and the former shall not be remembered, nor come into mind.

Isaiah 65:17, KJV

There the LORD will be our Mighty One. It will be like a place of broad rivers…

Isaiah 33:21a, NIV

Garden of the King

We find ourselves at the destination of our journey: the Prince's lands, in all their coming wonder. Along the way, there have been hints that Israel will truly be a garden-like country, with our Lord's land being at the apex of this beauty. Here in this closing chapter we will look at some of the reasons for this coming terrestrial paradise, and what it all might mean to us in the present.

Royal Foreshadowing

During his earlier regnal years of obedience and sanity[306], Solomon was the living foreshadow of Messiah to come[307]. In that capacity, he performed many wonderful works that included the following:

> *I made gardens and parks and planted all kinds of fruit trees in them. 6 I made reservoirs to water groves of flourishing trees.*
> *Ecclesiastes 2:5-6, NIV*

Solomon designed and made gardens, parks, orchards, lakes and watercourses. If his creations approached those of other emperors chronologically near him[308], and if the Temple and palaces he built are any indication, Solomon included many astounding features: crafted pathways, plazas, decorated walls, artistic embellishments and special plantings of botanic wonder everywhere.

Why did Solomon want gardens? In the Middle East, gardens had to be carefully designed in their water usage and planting arrangements, and were therefore very special places of rest, recreation, fellowship and intimacy. Ancient Biblical kings therefore had their private gardens[309]; and great kings would have truly great and elaborate ones. Without question, Solomon created wonderful environments for people to find repose amidst God's creation, in manicured settings fit for a king.

In addition to these more typical reasons for a royal garden, there was something else going on with Solomon. Without question, he took his gardens

---

[306] Ecclesiastes 2:9.

[307] As argued prior; see Matthew 12:42; Luke 11:31.

[308] For example, the garden of Xerxes described in Esther 1:5-6.

[309] E.g., 1 Kings 21:2; 2 Kings 21:18; Esther 1:5. 7:7-8; Nehemiah 3:15.

and parks seriously, counting them among his "great projects"[310]. Unlike other ancient kings though, this king did not simply delegate the gardening knowledge to others, but was personally adept in its workings.

> *He described plant life, from the cedar of Lebanon to the hyssop that grows out of walls…*
> *1 Kings 4:33a, NIV*
>
> *Solomon's knowledge of plant life was great enough to be listed as one of the reasons other kings sought him out:*
>
> *Men of all nations came to listen to Solomon's wisdom, sent by all the kings of the world, who had heard of his wisdom.*
> *1 Kings 4: 34, NIV*

Solomon, in many ways Jesus' prophetic forerunner, had vast knowledge of all things botanical, and had a passion for putting that knowledge into practice. As a "king of kings," Solomon had the means to do spectacular things in these regards.

In the Prince's coming Day, when the whole country is flowing with streams and blossoming with plant life, what might the King who is "greater than Solomon"[311] do? Will the Prince-King likewise take on such fascinating designs and constructions for his own "gardens and parks," with even more artistic aptitude, purpose, wisdom and energy? Surely, the Prince will perform no lesser than His "brother." More likely, He will conduct far more astounding projects – and all to the glory of God the Father.

Intimate Fellowship

Not only did an ancient king enjoy his gardens, but he did so with those close to them – and especially with his wife. As alluded to in a prior chapter, in the coming day Messiah will have been united with His own "bride," His people.

> *Let us rejoice and be glad and give him glory!* ***For the wedding of the Lamb has come, and his bride has made herself ready.*** *8 Fine linen, bright and clean, was given her to wear.*
> *Revelation 19:7-8, NIV*

310 Ecclesiastes 2:4.

311 Matthew 12:42; Luke 11:31.

The use of "bride" reflects the intensity of love that the Lord has toward us. In view of that passion, consider how closely Solomon associated his beloved with his private garden:

> *You are a* **garden** *locked up, my sister,* **my bride;** *you are a* **spring** *enclosed, a sealed fountain. 13 Your plants are an orchard of pomegranates with choice fruits, with henna and nard, 14 nard and saffron, calamus and cinnamon, with every kind of incense tree, with myrrh and aloes and all the finest spices. 15* **You are a garden fountain**, *a well of flowing water streaming down from Lebanon.*
> *Song of Solomon 4:12-15, NIV*

> *I have come into* **my garden**, *my sister,* **my bride;**
> *I have gathered my myrrh with my spice.*
> *I have eaten my honeycomb and my honey;*
> *I have drunk my wine and my milk.*
> *Song of Solomon 5:1, NIV*

Solomon uses his knowledge and love of plants and water to describe His beloved bride. Solomon's garden held the highest form of beauty to him, and was therefore the basis of his most intimate language. How all this relates in the Lord's day, only He fully comprehends. But we can at least dimly grasp that His love for His people is personal and intense, and that He intends to share His gardens with His beloved people-Bride.

The New Caretaker

Now, for a completely different perspective: *Adam.* With that first human, we also have the first occupation; and we see that the profession was not accidentally arrived at or backed into.

> *And the Lord God planted a* **garden** *eastward in Eden; and there he put the man whom he had formed... 15 And* **the Lord God took the man, and put him into the garden of Eden to dress it and to keep it.**
> *Genesis 2:8, KJV*

Before any disruption took place, this was the normal situation: Adam, and soon Eve, lived in this amazing garden and tended it. They ate from its bounty, and walked there with the Lord in "the cool of the day[312]." Before there

---

[312] Genesis 3:8.

was the "original sin," there was original beauty and divine perfection here on this Earth.

But since that sin, Earth's history was been a long recounting of the consequences of man's betrayal of the Lord. More importantly, the Bible displays the history of God's remedy in *ha Mashiach*, the Anointed. It is for good reason then that He is referred to as the Second Adam:

> *Nevertheless, death reigned from the time of Adam to the time of Moses, even over those who did not sin by breaking a command, as did* **Adam, who was a pattern of the one to come.** *15 But the gift is not like the trespass. For if the many died by the trespass of the one man, how much more did God's grace and the gift that came* **by the grace of the one man, Jesus Christ**, *overflow to the many! 16 Again, the gift of God is not like the result of the one man's sin: The judgment followed one sin and brought condemnation, but the gift followed many trespasses and brought justification. 17 For if, by the trespass of the one man, death reigned through that one man, how much more will those who receive God's abundant provision of grace and of the gift of righteousness reign in* **life through the one man, Jesus Christ**.
> *Romans 5:14-17, NIV*

> *So it is written: "The* **first man Adam** *became a living being";* **the last Adam, a life-giving spirit**. *46 The spiritual did not come first, but the natural, and after that the spiritual. 47* **The first man was of the dust of the earth, the second man from heaven.** *48 As was the earthly man, so are those who are of the earth; and as is the man from heaven, so also are those who are of heaven. 49 And just as we have borne the likeness of the earthly man, so shall we bear the likeness of* **the man from heaven.**
> *1 Corinthians 15:45-49, NIV*

In the Day coming, this "last Adam" will rule over the Earth. He is the "man from Heaven," and the very *Creator* of that original garden and all the rest of creation[313]. The "last Adam," the Prince, will have His own rich and well-watered lands. He will ensure that this new Eden, creation restored, is both well designed and well tended not only in His Province, but throughout His realms.

---

[313] E.g., Colossians 1:16.

Reversing the Curse

As we see in the creation story, this world remains under the original curse brought about by Satan's treachery and Adam's disobedience[314]. Man was disbarred from Eden; and creation was subjected to "thorns and thistles." In fact, the whole planet "groans" for a solution to this plight:

> ***The creation waits in eager expectation*** *for the sons of God to be revealed. 20 For the creation* ***was subjected to frustration****, not by its own choice, but by the will of the one who subjected it, in hope 21 that the* ***creation itself will be liberated from its bondage to decay and brought into the glorious freedom of the children of God.***
> *Romans 8:19-21. NIV*

Who is the forerunner to the resurrected and glorified "children of God"? The coming Caretaker of Eden, the second Adam who will remedy the original curse and overturn its cause:

> *For this purpose the Son of God was manifested, that* ***he might destroy the works of the devil.***
> *1 John 3:8b, KJV*

With the *apokalupsis*[315] or "revelation" of the Prince, there is by definition the commencement of this mighty rectification. It is His lands that are at the "epicenter" of the general natural rejuvenation so often prophesied.

> *For the land, whither thou goest in to possess it, is not as the land of Egypt, from whence ye came out, where thou sowedst thy seed, and wateredst it with thy foot, as a garden of herbs: But the land, whither ye go to possess it, is a land of hills and valleys, and drinketh water of the rain of heaven: 12* ***A land which the Lord thy God careth for:*** *the eyes of the Lord thy God are always upon it, from the beginning of the year even unto the end of the year. 13 And it shall come to pass, if* ***ye shall hearken diligently unto my commandments which I command you this day, to love the Lord your God, and to serve him with all your heart and with all your soul…***
> *Deuteronomy 11:10-13, KJV*

---

[314] Genesis 3.
[315] Strong's NT:602. The first word of the Book of *Revelation*, which gives that book its commonly-used title.

> *For the Lord shall comfort Zion:* **he will comfort all her waste places; and he will make her wilderness like Eden, and her desert like the garden of the Lord;** *joy and gladness shall be found therein, thanksgiving, and the voice of melody.*
> *Isaiah 51:3, KJV*

> *And the Lord shall guide thee continually, and satisfy thy soul in drought, and make fat thy bones: and* **thou shalt be like a watered garden, and like a spring of water, whose waters fail not.**
> *Isaiah 58:9, KJV*

> *I will greatly rejoice in the Lord, my soul shall be joyful in my God; for he hath clothed me with the garments of salvation, he hath covered me with the robe of righteousness, as a bridegroom decketh himself with ornaments, and as a bride adorneth herself with her jewels. 11* **For as the earth bringeth forth her bud, and as the garden causeth the things that are sown in it to spring forth; so the Lord God will cause righteousness and praise to spring forth before all the nations.**
> *Isaiah 61:10-11, KJV*

> *And they shall say,* **This land that was desolate is become like the garden of Eden;** *and the waste and desolate and ruined cities are become fenced, and are inhabited. 36 Then the heathen that are left round about you shall know that I the Lord build the ruined places, and plant that that was desolate: I the Lord have spoken it, and I will do it.*
> *Ezekiel 36:35-36, KJV*

> *And I will bring again the captivity of my people of Israel, and they shall build the waste cities, and inhabit them; and* **they shall plant vineyards, and drink the wine thereof; they shall also make gardens,** *and eat the fruit of them. 15* **And I will plant them upon their land, and they shall no more be pulled up out of their land** *which I have given them, saith the Lord thy God.*
> *Amos 9:14-15, KJV*

Though these are only a few of the numerous possible passages on the subject, they make things very clear. "Eden" will return and creation will be restored. And God's people, now fully obedient and loving, will enjoy the coming garden with Him.

Divine Resting Places

We began this Chapter with the subject of why kings enjoyed gardens, and why King Yeshua will surely have His. Now we can further look at why God (Father and Son) would have a garden. This coming "garden" of creation, particularly in the Prince's Province (and especially the Sacred District), is *God's* garden, made for *His* pleasure. We sense the divine enjoyment of original Eden: … *the Lord God walking in the garden in the cool of the day…* (Genesis 3:8b, KJV). And we can know He will enjoy this new Eden as well. Throughout this seventh[316] and thousand-year "day[317]," the Lord will have His Sabbath. He will obtain for Himself His Day of rest *within* this overall creation of His[318]; and "*His place of rest will be glorious*" (Isaiah 11:10).

Foretelling Features

In addition to creation's botanic renewal around the corner, related restorations in zoology[319], meteorology[320], and a number of other areas will coincide. But we have already seen the biggest "edenic" factor of all: the Lord Himself walking once more in His garden here on earth, with His people.

As for the natural elements of Eden, there is still more to the matter for our expedition, for within the Prince's lands are certain things that are particularly Eden-ish, far too obvious to be mere accident. Moreover, blended with these features are elements that clearly look forward to the final Paradise, the glorious eternal City.

The First Two Rivers

In original Eden's story there were four rivers involved, all originating from one mysteriously unnamed watercourse that emerged from within that garden.

---

[316] With a comparatively soon arrival of the Millennial era, Biblical dating makes it roughly the seventh one-thousand year period from Adam.

[317] Psalms 90:4; 2 Peter 3:8.

[318] E.g., Genesis 2:2-3.

[319] Based on, e.g., Isaiah 11 and 65.

[320] Based on, e.g., comparing the "firmament" of Genesis 1 with the "canopy" of Isaiah 4:5-6.

> ***And a river went out of Eden*** *to water the garden; and from thence it was parted, and became into four heads. 11 The name of the first is* ***Pison:*** *that is it which compasseth the whole land of Havilah, where there is gold; 12 And the gold of that land is good: there is bdellium and the onyx stone. 13 And the name of the second river is* ***Gihon:*** *the same is it that compasseth the whole land of Ethiopia. 14 And the name of the third river is* ***Hiddekel:*** *that is it which goeth toward the east of Assyria. And the fourth river is* ***Euphrates.***
> *Genesis 2:10-14, KJV*

Without question, much geological rearrangement has transpired since those days, making it almost impossible to say just how these rivers originally ran. However, we have seen one of them already: the Euphrates. We have seen that the coming borders of Israel will reach it, and can therefore see at least a reminiscence of Eden's rivers in this renewed garden of a country.

The Euphrates speaks to the northern border; and for the southern, we have already explored the "River of Egypt." Currently, it is a *wadi* of seasonal flow; then, it will capture much of the southern watershed of Israel, becoming a perpetual and mighty river in its own right. Does it correlate with any of the other three rivers of Eden? Not necessarily; and since it satisfies the purposes of symbolism (a river flowing explicitly from the new "Eden"), it doesn't need to.

Having said that, the Pishon went around the land of Havilah, which in later times was associated with Ishmaelites[321] and "Joktanic" Arabs[322]. Because of these connections with the Negev and other southern or wilderness areas, the River of Egypt (currently Wadi el-Arish) bears a strong connection with the prehistoric Pishon. If not literally, then it at least symbolically serves as another one of the four rivers emanating from future Eden-Israel.

The Second Two Rivers

As for the Hiddekel and Gihon, perhaps their watercourses are lost to time, memory and meaning. Or perhaps not. Arrangement-wise, we have seen two of the four: the river to the north (Euphrates) and the south (Pishon, or River of Egypt). And though Hiddekel's course is almost impossible to calculate based on present geography, it is associated with an eastward flow. That leaves Gihon, which is presumably associated with the remaining direction: westward.

So the question is, other than the northern and southern boundary-rivers, will there be *other* major rivers in Israel, perhaps linked to the Hiddekel and Gihon? First, consider the following hint:

---

321 Genesis 25:17-18.

322 Genesis 10:21.

> *Look upon Zion, the city of our festivals; your eyes will see Jerusalem, a peaceful abode, a tent that will not be moved; its stakes will never be pulled up, nor any of its ropes broken. 21* **There the LORD will be our Mighty One. It will be like a place of broad rivers and streams.** *No galley with oars will ride them, no mighty ship will sail them. 22 For the LORD is our judge, the LORD is our lawgiver, the LORD is our king; it is he who will save us.*
> *Isaiah 33:20-22, NIV*

Isaiah foresaw something quite literal[323], with the greater Jerusalem-Zion area characterized by great natural beauty, and marked often with streams, pools, lakes, waterfalls, and so on. It will also have rivers, and some of them will be quite large – large enough for the major classes of ship that Isaiah would have been familiar with. From a near-contemporary description[324], it is quite likely that ships on the scale of Phoenician galleys of 750-550 B.C. were in view for Isaiah. Even though they will be excluded, their wide beam and deep draft is telling: for a plurality (at least two) of these prophesied rivers of Jerusalem will be both wide and deep enough to accommodate such large watercraft.

Of these new watercourses, will there be an eastward and westward river associated with the land to come? Yes, and flowing through the Prince's eastern and western lands!

> *On that day living water will flow out from Jerusalem, half to the eastern sea and half to the western sea, in summer and in winter. 9 The LORD will be king over the whole earth. On that day there will be one LORD, and his name the only name.*
> *Zechariah 14:8-9, NIV*

> *On that day his [Messiah's] feet will stand on the Mount of Olives, east of Jerusalem, and the Mount of Olives will be split in two from east to west, forming a great valley, with half of the mountain moving north and half moving south. 5 You will flee by my mountain valley…*
> *Zechariah 14:4-5a, NIV*

Putting two and two together, we see a pair of rivers arising from Jerusalem, one flowing east, the other west. Enabled by the Mount of Olives split and resultant valley, the eastward river flows through the Prince's eastern land to the Jordan valley, turning south to the "eastern" (Dead) Sea. The westward river flows through His western lands, and on to the Mediterranean.

---

[323] The many technical nautical terms in his prophecy discount the notion of an entirely "symbolic" outworking.

[324] See Ezekiel 27:1-27.

Was Jerusalem ever connected with any of the rivers of Eden? Yes: the Gihon, a spring flowing into the Kidron Valley. In the coming day, the major river flowing to the west, big enough to support significant ancient vessels, may well be associated with Gihon, perhaps by name.

This leaves the other major river, flowing eastward and descending in what may involve quite dramatic waterfalls down to the Jordan Valley. Will it be called the Hiddekel? We aren't told. But from this new Eden, it will be a significant river, and the fourth that we can specifically identify.

The Fifth River

There is one more major river prophesied to flow within the Prince's lands to come. Unlike the four others, this one has no named counterpart in ancient Eden. Instead, it seems to have its roots in times far in the future. It is the mighty Temple River that commences from the throne of God in the Prince's Day[325]. To discuss it, we must take a small side trip, following the river's course from the His Province down to the Dead Sea.

This river originates from the Temple – from the top of the mount upon which it stands, that is, from near the center of the Sacred District's northern portion. Like the "Hiddekel" just south of it, this river flows eastward until it comes to the Jordan Valley[326], turns southward, and proceeds to the Dead Sea.

This river, however, is no ordinary one: for after a series of expansions[327] that Ezekiel carefully describes, its special properties are made clear:

> *He [the Lord] said to me, "This water flows toward the eastern region and goes down into the Arabah, where it enters the Sea. When it empties into the Sea, the water there becomes fresh. 9* **Swarms of living creatures will live wherever the river flows.** *There will be large numbers of fish, because this water flows there and makes the salt water fresh; so* **where the river flows everything will live.** *10 Fishermen will stand along the shore; from En Gedi to En Eglaim there will be places for spreading nets. The fish will be of many kinds — like the fish of the Great Sea.*
> *Ezekiel 47:8-10, NIV*

325 Ezekiel 47:1-12.

326 Since the Jordan Valley lies in the midst of the Prince's eastern land, the Temple River turns southward there (Ezekiel 47:8), and does not extend further through the eastern expanse of His property.

327 Presumably via the additive flow of other springs and streams along the way, all originating from the same aquifer system (e.g., Isaiah 30:25) that has the Temple Mount as chief of all the mountains (Isaiah 2:2; Micah 4:1) contributing to that phenomenon.

Through the basic and most ancient occupation of fishing, the Lord shows us much about this wonderful river. Like any fresh-water river entering a salt-water body, there will be a transition zone of impact. We call such zones 'brackish,' a mix of salt water and fresh. But something different is happening here: the river's waters will keep a significant portion of the Dead Sea's waters distinctly fresh. As a result, huge numbers of fish, mainly of fresh-water species, and other aquatic creatures, will be present.

Keep in mind that the Dead Sea, salty and "dead" in ancient times as it was, is especially dying on our present day. Its coastlines have retreated dramatically; its shores at some points are a wasteland in comparison with only decades ago; and its salt concentration only increases. It would take a *lot* of water for this deadest of seas, *the lowest place on earth*, to be restored as a virile body of water. And it would take a miraculous introduction of *fresh* water for big swarms of aquatic creatures to survive and even flourish there.

Because of the Temple River though, the Bible declares that this will indeed be the case. It will have such dramatic effect that fishermen will be able to haul huge catches on at least the western shore of the Dead Sea. With this reversal of the Dead Sea's fortunes, it is clear the Creator remains the ultimate proponent of His creation. It is also clear that, from this "humblest" (elevationally lowest) example, He will perform similarly astounding things throughout the entire world He created.

There is another "fish story" here though, and it leads to even bigger things. Notice that the fish of the Dead Sea will be "*like the fish of the Great Sea.*" This is a reference to the Mediterranean and – to the ancients of the Bible – to the oceans in general. Therefore two biological points are being made by our main guide, Ezekiel. First, that the fresh-water creatures (at the northern and western edges of the Dead Sea, at the minimum) will become quite large. Second, we see that salt-water creatures in the remainder of that body of water will also flourish, and likewise be able to grow to large size[328]. The impact of the "Temple River" on aquatic life here will be so astounding that a new name will surely be needed – perhaps simply "the Eastern Sea"[329].

These fish will serve as but one example of God's life-giving healing to all creation then. For the main point in Ezekiel's passage is this: "***living creatures***

---

[328] To the marine biologist, such matters might seem puzzling for a sea that has no outlet. The solution may lie, however, in certain prophecies that perhaps indicate an opening of the Jordan Valley to the Gulf of Aqaba and the Red Sea – without which the huge flow of the Temple River would have no exit, and presumably cause flooding. The first such prophetic indication was that large ships *could* have navigated here, but will not be permitted to. The second is that "the LORD shall utterly destroy the tongue of the Egyptian sea" (Isaiah 11:15, KJV), indicating major tectonic activity in the Sinai Peninsula, and thus, most likely, in the related Jordan Rift Valley fault system.

[329] Ezekiel 47:18; Joel 2:20; Zechariah 14:8.

will live wherever the river flows." [330] This may be an oblique reference to, and a mighty expression of, that initial (but unnamed) river that fed Eden in Genesis 2:10, and thereafter split into the four others. More explicitly, this is nothing less than a gigantic precursor to the *eternal* River of Life:

> *And he shewed me a pure river of water of life, clear as crystal, proceeding out of the throne of God and of the Lamb.*
> *Revelation 22:1, KJV*

Before that final and mightiest River flows, there will be this astounding precursor in Messiah's day. Like the final one, this life-giving River will emanate from the throne of God, His coming Temple [331]. Like the final one, its foreshadowing will be said to bring life wherever it flows, to whatever it touches. While the other four rivers hark back to original Eden and what God performed in the past, this one reaches forward to *eternal* Eden and what He will do in the future. At the same time, it can be said that ancient Eden, eternal Paradise, and the garden on our horizon all have this mighty river that is named only for the fact that it flows with God's own life in its waters.

Nourishing Trees

With this most mysterious of future Israel's primary rivers, there is another fascinating property. This river, along with two others, is described by the Bible as having a very special tree involved. Original Eden's unnamed river watered that garden and flowed from it, subsequently dividing into the four major headwaters discussed earlier [332]. Associated with that "river of life" was the original and singular Tree of Life. At the other end of the Biblical prophetic spectrum, the eternal City's River of Life is flanked by numerous instances of that same Tree [333]. In between original Eden and Eternal Eden, here in this coming Messianic realm and era, we have a similar pairing of these two great features of tree and river:

> *He asked me, "Son of man, do you see this?" Then he led me back to the bank of the river. 7 When I arrived there, I saw a great number of trees on each side of the river. "...Fruit trees of all kinds will grow on both banks of the river. Their leaves will not wither, nor will their fruit fail. Every month they will bear, because the water*

330 Ezekiel 47:9.
331 Ezekiel 47:1.
332 Genesis 2:10-14.
333 Revelation 22:2.

> *from the sanctuary flows to them. Their fruit will serve for food and their leaves for healing."*
> *Ezekiel 47:6-7 & 12, NIV*

Compare these special Millennial trees (and their life-giving capacities) with those of the eternal City:

> *Then the angel showed me the river of the water of life, as clear as crystal, flowing from the throne of God and of the Lamb 2 down the middle of the great street of the city. On each side of the river stood the tree of life, bearing twelve crops of fruit, yielding its fruit every month. And the leaves of the tree are for the healing of the nations.*
> *Revelation 22:1-2, NIV*

How similar these arrangements are! Just as with the Eternal City, the Millennial River from the coming "throne" of God will be flanked by healing trees. Growing all along its banks are trees resembling – in appearance and in effect – both the Tree of Life with which Adam was first confronted, and the "forest" of Trees of Life in *eternal* Jerusalem.

Though Adam was prevented from eating of the first Tree of Life, the Second Adam, Jesus, will bring His people to these coming instances of it and encourage their partaking. Just as in the final setting with the eternal City, their fruit and leaves will be fully accessible for the nourishment and healing of all God's children. Moreover, these marvelous Millennial trees, blatantly symbolizing the eternal Trees of Life, will loudly signify that mortality will soon be abolished, in entirety, forever and ever.

There are practical ramifications here for the Prince's land: for as Ezekiel simply puts it, "*their fruit will serve as food.*" People of Israel and all nations will come to enjoy this very literal fruit, perhaps detecting a distinctly eternal "flavor" to it. But it will not be only one fruit. In what Ezekiel and John *both* foresaw, these trees are of a species unknown to us now: for they bring forth a different fruit on each particular month. Month after month, year after year, this will be a perpetual cycle of differing tastes and textures, with these fruits being enjoyed on a continual and year-round process.

Announcing the fruit of the Tree of Life for all eternity to come, and perhaps echoing the manna of the wilderness journey, the Lord will offer this very special food to His subjects that seek it. Himself being the Bread of Life[334], only the Prince is the appropriate one to own the very holy land upon which these trees grow, and to grant the holy food of life in their fruit.

[334] John 6.

Healing Trees

There is another important function of these same trees, in that their leaves are distinctly meant for healing. For the Millennial "trees of life": ***"Their leaves will not wither...their leaves... will serve... for healing."*** For the eternal Trees of Life: ***"And the leaves of the tree are for the healing of the nations."*** The first serve as the symbol for the final; and in both, we see healing.

Why the need for healing? For the Eternal City, we are not informed of what "injuries" might be the candidates. But in Messiah's time, physical healing will still have a hugely important role, and we can cite several examples here. Though not the intended outcome of the Lord's, people will indeed die during this next age[335], indicating that healthcare would have been probably sought prior. In attaining great age, especially toward the end of the Millennial period (and in view of the fact that aging will occur[336]), the elderly may well require certain remedies. As another example, women will regularly give birth[337], and certain cases may not go as perfectly as the norm. Also, even though great longevity will be the pattern, the prophecies do not guarantee the world's citizens against instances of simple injury[338]. Lastly, certain peoples may attempt to rebel[339], see a negative physical result, and – upon reflection – seek very much the Lord's restoration of their physical health.

Hence, the continued need for physical healing in the Prince's day. For those future healing activities, it is fascinating to see that the means is already accounted for in the prophecies, in the the *leaves* of those same trees. It is not only their fruit that is efficacious in a "life-giving" regard, but also their healing leaves. Never disappearing in the winter months, this wonderful source will be available to the Prince's world-wide constituency all year long, every year. Since the leaves do not wither, they may well stay fresh during transport to far-flung places. For the implication is that, as a healing means, they may be brought to those that are bed-ridden. A very different, and wonderful, form of healthcare indeed!

Beyond all the wonders of the coming Garden, there stands the "Gardener," the Creator, the final Adam: for it will be Messiah, Son of David, who enables and orchestrates all these things. He is the "firstfruits[340]" of all

---

[335] Isaiah 65:20.

[336] Ibid.

[337] As is seen in the several instances of very young children being present in that time, and as an ongoing factor (e.g., Isaiah 11:6 & 8).

[338] Though, thankfully, not due to war (e.g., Micah 4:3).

[339] Though not mentioning personal injury, Zechariah 14:7-9 implies that some will rebel, with bad results to their rainfall – and presumably other aspects of life. The huge instance of such rebellion is *after* the Messianic era, described in Revelation 20:7-9.

[340] 1 Corinthians 15:20, 23.

eternal humankind, the ultimate man[341] whose proven holiness is that of God Himself. So perhaps there is more than meets the eye in the opening Psalm composed by His maternal "father," David:

> ***He is like a tree planted by streams of water, which yields its fruit in season and whose leaf does not wither. Whatever he does prospers.***
> *Psalms 1:3, NIV*

When all is said and done, Jesus is that ultimate "tree," for which all these trees of life are emblematic. He is the "vine" from whence all our life and prospering comes[342], and the source of healing for all the nations and families of mankind, throughout eternity.

Looking Forward

As we wrap up our expedition, let's take a step back and briefly compare what we have seen with the larger settings.

Eden's Crescendo

The prophecies of God's Word always emphasize Israel, for it is the country He chose to demonstrate His mighty redemptive plan, and the home of the people He first chose to work through. Therefore we have seen a wealth of information on how Israel, and especially the Prince's Province and Jerusalem, will be garden-like in His coming Day. This does not, however, exclude the rest of the world from being similarly blessed. With the original curse having been remedied, its maladies removed, and all creation being unfettered[343], the global blessing will be unimaginable.

> *For, behold, I create new heavens and a new earth: and the former shall not be remembered, nor come into mind.*
> *Isaiah 65:17, KJV*

341 In Hebrew, '*adam.*'
342 John 15:1-8.
343 Romans 8:21-23.

Not surprisingly, something very similar is said for the eternal Heaven-with-Earth creation[344]. But as its precursor in this present creation, the Lord is here speaking specifically of the period prior, the one on the horizon[345], the Millennial Day of the Lord. Armed with that fact, let's appreciate what Isaiah conveys: that the entire world and all its skies ('heavens') will be so wonderful and new that the former will not be at all comparable. The "*former*" is the world we inhabit right now! So even in view of all the natural wonders one can experience in this world today, the coming *renewed* version, with the curse taken away and all created life freed to reach the original potential, will be all the more breathtaking.

These "edenic" conditions and blessings will therefore be world-wide. Even so, Israel will be the special recipient, and the lands of the Prince-King even more so. So while we should think of this coming Eden as global, we should also understand that it has a crescendo of sorts, gradually building to the ultimate center, the Sacred District within the Prince's lands.

> ***Many nations*** *will come and say, "Come, let us go up to the mountain of the Lord, to the house of the God of Jacob. He will teach us his ways, so that we may walk in his paths." The law will go out from Zion, the word of the Lord from Jerusalem. 3 He will judge between* **many peoples** *and will settle disputes for* **strong nations far and wide.** *They will beat their swords into plowshares and their spears into pruning hooks. Nation will not take up sword against nation, nor will they train for war anymore. 4* **Every man will sit under his own vine and under his own fig tree**, *and no one will make them afraid, for the Lord Almighty has spoken.*
> *Micah 4:2-4, NIV*[346]

Families and peoples all around the world will peacefully enjoy their individual "vine and fig tree" blessings, and tend their own gardens, whether literally or figuratively. But the ultimate garden will be under the care of our culminating Adam, creation's Creator, Yeshua-Jesus. It is He whose "*law will go out from Zion, the word of the Lord from Jerusalem.*" Under the Prince of Peace, all the world will flourish. Yet the greatest expression of that prosperity, and most garden-like conditions, will be on God's Mountain, *Zion.*

---

[344] Revelation 21:12; cf Peter 3:13.

[345] Amongst other Millennial-only factors, the passage describes the recent extraction and gathering of newly-repentant Israel, and the remaining phenomena of childbirth, aging and death.

[346] See also Isaiah 2:3-4.

Eden's Practice

As nature's wonders will build towards the center of "Eden," so too will worship.

> *The Lord will be awesome to them when he destroys all the gods of the land.* ***The nations on every shore will worship him, every one in its own land.***
> *Zephaniah 2:9*

> ***Many nations will come and say, "Come, let us go up to the mountain of the Lord, to the house of the God of Jacob.*** *He will teach us his ways, so that we may walk in his paths."*
> *Micah 4:2a, NIV*

Though the practices of this worldwide worship are not detailed in Scripture, we see that all nations will worship the Lord God in their own lands. We see that all will share an urge[347] to come to Zion, the Holy Mountain within the Sacred District and at the center of Eden to come. We also know that the Word of God remains central[348], and that true worship of Him is in spirit[349]. In that coming Day then, people just like you and I will live in restored creation, journey to Eden's center, hear with their own ears the teaching of the Prince, and blend their voices in the perpetual and global worship of God Almighty.

Today, we do not have Eden's evidences; but we have natural fragments so astounding that they unequivocally declare God's wonder and glory[350]. Today, we cannot make pilgrimage to the place of the King's rest; but we can enter that very same rest and peace of His own[351]. Today, we cannot physically walk with the Prince; but we can in spirit, and do so in all aspects and situations of our lives[352]. Today, we cannot physically speak with the coming King; but in prayer, we can[353], and converse with Him as effectually as if we were bodily in the same room.

It is thrilling to look into the Lord's coming physical realm on Earth as we have done here, and the glimpse can encourage our faith. However, our union with our God is first in spirit, and our original purpose is to walk with Him, in His garden. These things have never changed, nor will they. So while circumstances now might seem bland and even ugly, the Lord is always inviting

---

347 See Zechariah 8:23.
348 Matthew 24:35; Mark 13:31; Luke 21:33.
349 John 4:24; Philippians 3:3.
350 E.g., Psalms 19:1, 97:6; Romans 1:20.
351 E.g., Philippians 4:6-7; Hebrews 4:3-11.
352 E.g., Psalms 86:11, 116:9; John 8:12; 2 Corinthians 6:16 (quoting Leviticus 26:12).
353 E.g., Psalms 55:22, 62:8; Proverbs 3:5-6; Matthew 7:7; Philippians 4:6-7.

us. He calls us to join Him, to enter His rest, to walk with Him in a secret garden to which He alone holds the key.

Eden's Deepening

Thanks to our guide Ezekiel, and many other ancient servants of the Lord, we have been granted a very present vision of the future country of Messiah and of the first-chosen nation, Israel. Though our expedition has been in advance of the outworking, the Word assures us that it will be as real as any land we might journey to today. The Lord has invited us to a glimpse of that land's reality, by His Word and Spirit, and we have attempted it.

In the effort, we have also seen that one province stands profoundly unique: that belonging to the Prince-King to come, a region set amongst all Israel's tribal portions. In the center of that Province, we have also noticed the most sacred plot of land in the entire world on the horizon: the Sacred District. Deeper still, that holy district will contain the capitol City of the King, Jerusalem. Just as importantly, also contained will be the "house" of the Name of the Lord: the vast Temple.

Ever expanding, the further story of coming "Eden" will proceed in deeper layers of wonder, building toward that Temple at its center, and even beyond.

But those are further journeys.

In the mean time, it is my hope that you have been as encouraged in your faith as I have, in the expedition we have taken there. Like our "father" in faith, Abraham, we look to that coming City. Regardless of where we are on God's timeline, we seek His kingdom now in Heaven, but yet is coming to this creation. As the Prince commanded us to pray, and we do often, "***Thy kingdom come.*** *Thy will be done in earth,* **as it is in heaven**[354]**."**

And so it shall be.

---

354 Matthew 6:10, KJV; also Luke 11:2.

Appendix A: Firstborn's Portion

The Law of the Firstborn

The Nation-Man

In discussing expansions to the Holy Land in Messiah's day (Chapter 3), it was pointed out that the "law of the firstborn" may come into play, granting an additional confirmation to other factors of enlargement.

Many times the Bible refers to an ancient nation as if it were an individual person[355]. As but one example:

> *Listen to me, O house of Jacob, all you who remain of the house of Israel, you whom I have upheld since you were conceived, and have carried since your birth. Even to your old age and gray hairs I am he, I am he who will sustain you. I have made you and I will carry you; I will sustain you and I will rescue you.*
> *Isaiah 46:3-4, NIV*

From such passages, we are reminded that a particular ethnic people originated from a God-chosen and God-created ancestor. We are also reminded that God remains just as sovereign over the descendants, no matter how plentiful, as He was over the patriarch.

---

[355] E.g., Israel, Moab, Ammon, and Edom.

The Legal Imperative

Next, we should understand the ancient Biblical rights of the literal firstborn son, and to look to the Law of Moses to see how God upholds that son's rights[356], even when circumstances might argue otherwise:

> *If a man has two wives, and he loves one but not the other, and both bear him sons but the firstborn is the son of the wife he does not love, when he wills his property to his sons, he must not give the rights of the firstborn to the son of the wife he loves in preference to his actual firstborn , the son of the wife he does not love.* ***He must acknowledge*** *the son of his unloved wife as* ***the firstborn by giving him a double share of all he has. That son is the first sign of his father's strength. The right of the firstborn belongs to him.***
> *Deuteronomy 21:15-17, NIV*

Notice the reason for this special blessing: because the firstborn is "the first sign of his father's strength." We will come back to that point in a moment. For now, we see that the father must acknowledge the firstborn, and give him a "double share." And we can also observe that this is a law that obligates the father, rather than the son.

Now, the "nation-man" Israel bears a unique distinction amongst all the nations, for "he" is actually considered by God as His "firstborn son."

> *Then say to Pharaoh, 'This is what the LORD says:* ***Israel is my firstborn son****, and I told you,* ***"Let my son go****, so he may worship me." But you refused to let him go; so I will kill your firstborn son." '*
> *Exodus 4:22-23, NIV*

> *They will come with weeping; they will pray as I bring them back. I will lead them beside streams of water on a level path where they will not stumble,* ***because I am Israel's father, and Ephraim[357] is my firstborn son.***
> *Jeremiah 31:9, NIV*

Father-God has showed His love and mercy toward all peoples, throughout all history. However, the "man" Israel, *as a nation*, was the initial recipient of this Divine interaction, and therefore the first "sign" of God's strength, His redemptive power. Thus God can still refer to the nation of Israel as His "firstborn son," and be glorified in doing so.

---

[356] Sometimes the exception proves the rule, seen in God choosing Jacob over his (slightly) older brother Esau (Edom).

[357] The tribe of Ephraim, due to its dominance, was representative of all the northern tribes, and therefore the bulk of Israel at the time.

Tying these elements together, we can see that Israel, as "firstborn" of God's redeemed peoples, has special legal rights amongst other nations.

An Enduring Right

Adding to the equation, we just read about another fascinating factor, relating to status of the mother of the firstborn (see Deuteronomy 21:15, cited above). The right of the firstborn endures, even if the father no longer loves his mother. Again, this is an obligation upon the father to acknowledge the firstborn, regardless of other conditions.

This is a vital point, speaking to the argument that God "divorced" Israel. The Bible sometimes speaks of Israel as being the "wife" of the Lord, and He as her husband[358]. However, there was a time when that nation so angered God that He figuratively "*gave faithless Israel her certificate of divorce and sent her away because of all her adulteries*" (Jeremiah 3:8). So on the one hand, ancient Israel was seen as the "wife of God" that He was furious with, and even "divorced." On the other hand, the descendents of Jacob remain, as a people, God's "firstborn son."

In view of the law of the firstborn, and the important provisions of Deuteronomy 21:15, the offenses of the "mother" cannot take away from the inheritance of the "son." So no matter how many relational difficulties there have been between ancestral Israel (as a nation) and the Lord (her "Husband"), the inheritance rights for "her offspring" remain undisturbed; the right of the firstborn nation-son remains in force.

Applying the Doubling

When Messiah affirms, assigns and clarifies land-inheritances for all peoples in the future, Jacob-Israel will again stand in a unique position. As God's firstborn nation-son, and regardless of issues of the past, the law demands that a "double share" be granted.

---

358 E.g., Jeremiah 3:14.

The Doubling Confirmed

In case there is any doubt, and in addition to the Law of the Firstborn, we have an explicit statement that confirms a doubling of property for Israel to come:

> *And you will be called priests of the LORD, you will be named ministers of our God. You will feed on the wealth of nations, and in their riches you will boast. 7 Instead of their shame* **my people will receive a double portion**, *and instead of disgrace they will rejoice in their* **inheritance;** *and so* **they will inherit a double portion in their land,** *and everlasting joy will be theirs.*
> *Isaiah 61:6-7, NIV*

What then is this "double portion," and how does it relate to what we've seen so far? Is it some metaphor for a vague blessing of another sort? No! It is a direct reference to the undeniable inheritance rights of the firstborn. And when applied on a national scale, this principle of doubling the legacy translates to a simple doubling of territory.

So now we see why, in a time when Israel will enjoy "the wealth of nations" as "priests of the Lord," God has declared that His "firstborn" nation will see "his" territory approximately doubled.

What is the Baseline?

But "doubling" in comparison to *what*? Isaiah does not say. But for the sake of argument, would Ezekiel's borders effectively double Israel's *present* land holdings? The area of Israel is 20,770 km^2 (8,019 mi^2) in its contemporary configuration[359], and about 52,107 km^2 (20,119 mi^2) in its Ezekiel 47:15-19 configuration. That's about 2.5 times larger. Without question, the prophesied real estate would easily "double" Israel's present holdings.

---

359 Per the CIA database, May 5 2013, <https://www.cia.gov/library/publications/the-world-factbook/geos/is.html>.

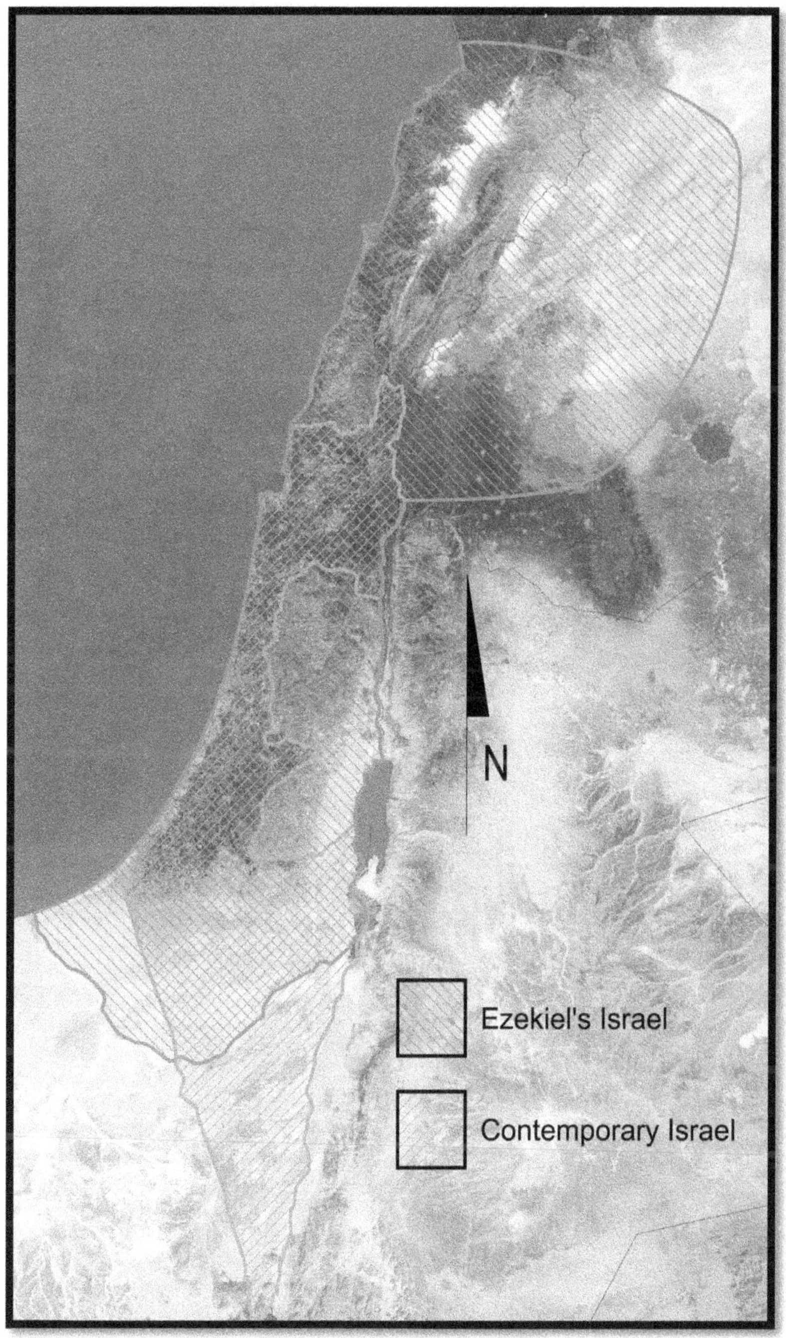

Figure 22: A Border Comparison

So while it is an interesting comparison to make, are today's boundaries of Israel (with major regions gouged out and ever more land being demanded in exchange for "peace") really the thing God had in mind when He spoke about this "doubling" through Isaiah? No, because God's intended provisions for His "firstborn" do not change with the vicissitudes of human politics and alterations of historical boundaries. Israel's borders have changed a lot, even in recent decades; and we can expect more of the same. So instead of that rather fluid basis, there must be a more solid starting point for a calculation of future area.

A Better Basis for Doubling

Fortunately, the baseline for this doubled "inheritance" is firmly established by other means. When God Almighty created the original (seventy) nations[360], He assigned a land to each of them:

> *When* **the Most High gave the nations their inheritance**, *when he divided all mankind,* **he set up boundaries for the** *peoples according to the number of the sons of Israel.*
> *Deuteronomy 32:8, NIV*

> *From one man he made every nation of men, that they should inhabit the whole earth; and* **he determined** *the times set for them and* **the exact places where they should live.** *27 God did this so that men would seek him and perhaps reach out for him and find him, though he is not far from each one of us.*
> *Acts 17:26-27, NIV*

These original holdings were considered the legacy for each nation. Their "*boundaries*" for "*the exact places where they should live*" were not determined at random, not by wars over time, but by the Lord as the masterful assigner of each particular "inheritance" for each major people-group[361].

Now, Israel was not among those first nations, but was instead *extracted* from the other nations as *God's* inheritance[362]. When doing so, He created for them a new territory-basis and land inheritance[363], just as valid as that granted to any other nation on the face of the earth.

---

360 Genesis 10.

361 Note that the Hebrew term *nachala* (Strong's 5159), translated "inheritance," is generally associated with real estate.

362 E.g., Deuteronomy 4:20; Psalms 33:12, 106:5; Joel 2:17, 3:2.

363 E.g., Exodus 32:13; Leviticus 20:24; Numbers 34:1; Deuteronomy 12:10; Joshua 11:23.

When was *that* guaranteed legacy first specifically granted? Through Moses. In regards to the "doubling" in the law of the firstborn, to what does the term "inheritance" refer here? Those same original borders, as laid down by Moses and (much later) affirmed through Ezekiel.

What this means is that Israel, in Messiah's day, will most likely occupy not only the approximately 52,107 km^2 (20,119 mi^2) area described by Moses and Ezekiel, but a region having about *twice that area.*

This doubled inheritance will bring great joy to Jacob's descendents in that day, just as the prophets foretold. But it will also honor to the Lord Himself, for it will acknowledge His strength working through Israel in history past, and especially in the day of His coming Kingdom.

Selected Bibliography

Beitzel, Barry J. The Moody Atlas of Bible Lands.
Chicago, IL: Moody Publishers, Inc., 2000.

Gundry, Robert H. The Church and the Tribulation: A Biblical Examination of Posttribulationism.
Grand Rapids, MI: Zondervan Publishing House, 1973.

Ladd, George Eldon. A Commentary on the Revelation of John.
Grand Rapids, MI: Eerdmans Publishing Company, 1972.

Orr, James, ed. International Standard Bible Encyclopedia (ISBE).
Grand Rapids, MI: Eerdmans Publishing Company, 1939.

PC Study Bible
Seattle, WA: Biblesoft.

About the Author

Cliff Jennings lives near Baltimore, Maryland with his wife Linda, and they are the proud parents of Rebecca, Hunter, Leah and Bethany. Cliff is a mechanical design-engineer who enjoys studies in Biblical prophecy, particularly from a technical perspective.

If you would like to learn more about further work in this book series, or give feedback on what you've read here, please visit our website: www.EarthAwaits.com.

www.ingramcontent.com/pod-product-compliance
Lightning Source LLC
Chambersburg PA
CBHW021927040426
42448CB00008B/940

* 9 7 8 0 9 9 0 3 8 9 4 0 8 *